THE
PERFUMED GARDEN
OF SENSUAL DELIGHT

The Perfumed Garden of Sensual Delight has a bad reputation and a tattered history. For over a century, it has been known in English through Sir Richard Burton's bizarre translation (from the French) which consistently elaborated and misrepresented the original. If ever a book needed demystifying, it is this one. Although remarkably lewd at times, it does not linger over details nor does it contrive to excite. It does not, therefore, qualify as pornography. In fact, *The Perfumed Garden of Sensual Delight* is nothing more than a manual for the ordinary, married man of its author's time and place – Tunisia, in the early part of the 15th century – but one that is not without some entertainment value.

The present translation is not only the first, published English version to be based upon an established Arabic text, but also the first to be translated directly from the original Arabic at all.

JIM COLVILLE has wide experience throughout the Middle East and North Africa as an Arabic/English translator and interpreter. He is currently with the Royal Commission in Jubail, Saudi Arabia.

THE PERFUMED GARDEN
OF SENSUAL DELIGHT
(ar-rawd al-'âṯir fî nuzhati'l khâṯir)

by

Muhammad ibn Muhammad al-Nafzawi

Translated from the Arabic
with a short introduction and notes

by

Jim Colville

THE ROUTLEDGE ARABIA LIBRARY
VOLUME SEVEN

Routledge
Taylor & Francis Group

LONDON AND NEW YORK

First published in 1999 by
Routledge
2 Park Square, Milton Park, Abingdon, Oxon, OX14 4RN
711 Third Avenue, New York, NY 10017

Transferred to Digital Printing 2011

ISBN10: 0-7103-0644-X (hbk)
ISBN10: 0-4156-0589-X (pbk)
ISBN13: 978-0-7103-0644-9 (hbk)
ISBN13: 978-0-4156-0589-2 (pbk)

British Library Cataloguing in Publication Data
Ibn Muhammad al-Nafzawi, Muhammad
The perfumed garden of sensual delight. – (the Routledge
Arabia library)
1. Husbands - Tunisia 2. Tunisia - Social life and customs
I. Title II. Colville, Jim
305.3'1'09611'09024
ISBN 071030644X

Library of Congress Cataloging-in-Publication Data
Applied for

Publisher's Note
The publisher has gone to great lengths to ensure the quality of this reprint
but points out that some imperfections in the original may be apparent.

CONTENTS

INTRODUCTION

This little book has a bad reputation and a tattered history. Discovered around the middle of the nineteenth century by the cultural wing of the occupying French army in North Africa, it was brought to Europe, suitably dressed for the occasion, and displayed in limited editions as an example of *l'orientalisme exotique* so much in vogue at the time. However, the nineteenth century European invention of the Orient suggests nothing more exotic than a caricature of its own fantasy in which *The Perfumed Garden*, among others, was coerced into the role of surrogate. Indeed, the book's treatment provides a striking example of what has been called "the seductive degradation of knowledge."[1] That it has played an unwitting role in shaping European views of Arab cultural and social values is clear:

> It is largely due to his [al-Nafzawi's] book, and to Burton's masterly [*sic*] translation of the *Arabian Nights*, that the West has come to a reasonably precise, accurate, and systematised knowledge of Mohammedan sexual life and thought.[2]

Perhaps better to have left well alone in the first place but the least that can now be done, by way of contrition, is to provide a faithful translation – something that, in English, *The Perfumed Garden* has conspicuously lacked.

The book deals with sex in an open and uninhibited way; it is, by turns, serious and amusing, almost sublime and quite ridiculous. Sin and shame are specifically excluded from this garden, where sexual pleasure is a divine gift we all have the right to enjoy. Although remarkably lewd at times (so lewd it is almost cathartic), *The Perfumed Garden* does not linger gratuitously over details nor does it contrive to excite. It does not, therefore, qualify as pornography – as I hope readers of this translation will

---

[1] E. Said, *Orientalism*, (London, Penguin: 1995), p. 328

[2] Sir R. Burton (trans.), *The Perfumed Garden of the Shaykh Nefzawi*, edited with an Introduction by A. H. Walton, (London, Panther: 1963), Introduction, pp. 8-9

agree. The stories and poems create a thin literary veneer but hardly give it the character of a work of literature. None are likely to be original and many would have been familiar, in one form or another, to al-Nafzawi's readers. Neither is the book a treatise on sexuality; two stories featuring lesbians and a joke about a donkey suggest no more than, at most, casual interest in the spectrum of sexual inclination. This is the misunderstanding that left earlier translators so dissatisfied with the original. *The Perfumed Garden* is a practical guide for the ordinary married man.

The book has not fared well in Arabic-speaking countries either. Until recently, and despite the existence of a number of manuscript copies, the only published edition was a dismal, error-ridden version produced, it appears, in response to the curiosity aroused by European interest. The title is familiar to many but the book is known to few, not least in the land of its author's birth.

*

Of Abu 'Abdullah Muhammad ibn Muhammad al-Nafzawi, very little is known with certainty. His name suggests an origin in the south of what is now Tunisia, from the homeland of the Nefzaoua tribe near the town of Kebili, or perhaps, with less likelihood, in the far north of that country, from the town of Nefza. His dates of birth and death, profession and other details of his life are obscure.

However, he tells us in his preface to *The Perfumed Garden* that it was written at the request of one Muhammad ibn 'Awana al-Zawawi, appointed chief minister to the Sultan of Tunis, 'Abdalaziz al-Hafsi, after the latter's seizure of Algiers. Abu Faris 'Abdalaziz al-Hafsi was a distinguished scion of the Hafsid dynasty of Tunis (1228-1574) whose own period of rule (1394-1434) was a time of territorial expansion and material prosperity. He captured the city of Algiers in 1410 or 1411 and, the same year, appointed his friend Muhammad ibn 'Abdalaziz as chief minister – an arrangement that held until the Sultan's death in 1434.[3] If we may assume that Muhammad ibn 'Awana and Muhammad ibn 'Abdalaziz are one and the same, we may conclude that al-Nafzawi wrote *The Perfumed Garden* sometime between 1410/1411 and 1434. It is unlikely he was a resident of Tunis, given the information in the preface that

---

[3] R. Brunschvig, *La Berbérie orientale sous les Hafsides*, 2 vols., (Paris: 1940, 1947), vol. I, p. 210 ff.

his audience with Muhammad ibn 'Awana took place after having enjoyed three days of hospitality subsequent to arrival at his residence.[4]

*

Present-day Arab opinion of *The Perfumed Garden* is divided. There are those who appreciate the candid and open treatment of so private a subject as the physical relationship between man and wife and, in recent years, a scholarly interest in this aspect of mediaeval writing has developed. But there is also regret at its populist style and evidently downmarket appeal. It is of uneven quality and at times repetitive. There is also criticism of its medical advice (although al-Nafzawi's prescriptions are not superstitions). However, the principal target of Arab criticism is not so much the book itself but the choice of a book of this kind to represent Arabo-Muslim culture and further, the consistent misrepresentation of that choice. It is not an understatement to note that, stripped of acquired mystique, *The Perfumed Garden* hardly lays claim to greatness.

The book may be criticised, too, from other quarters. It is written exclusively for men and assumes the desirability of polygamy. Women are presented as liable to so many more physical and character defects than men (a casual reading suggests that all a man needs to be concerned about is the size of his penis and his inherent gullibility). Betrayal and deception of their husbands seems to be the order of the day and older women, in particular, get hard treatment. Many of the book's assumptions were not, of course, uncommon in contemporary Europe.

Romantic love carries a grave health warning in *The Perfumed Garden* but is not examined in any depth. It will be tactless to pursue al-Nafzawi on this point. The great Andalusian scholar Ibn Hazm, who preceded him by some four hundred years, dealt with the psychology of love and lovers with a peerless profundity and refinement in his *The Collar of the Dove*.[5]

However, if we accept the book's obvious limitations, we are free to look objectively at and approve of its positive elements. It displays a

---

[4] I am aware of no external sources of information on al-Nafzawi's life. A reference by Ibn Battuta, in his *Travels*, to a meeting at Tunis in the early 1320s with a jurist with a similar name to our author's can be discounted, given that its date is inconsistent with what al-Nafzawi himself tells us.
[5] English translation by A. J. Arberry (London: 1953)

concern with integrity while encouraging a sense of fun and lack of inhibition. It stresses physical and temperamental compatibility between a man and wife and highlights matters of health and personal hygiene. It recognises the importance of arousal through foreplay, of pleasure for both partners and of orgasm for a woman (albeit motivated by a belief in the unlikelihood of conception unless both partners climax simultaneously).

The book's longer stories have the character of folk-tales. The story of Bahloul and Hamdouna in Chapter One – still current, with variations, in Tunisia today – is a minor classic of wit and, after a rather shaky start, Chapter Two's tale about the king's discovery of the brothel depicts a hard core of disillusioned realism. Respectively, these stories present the ambiguous and not wholly fictitious character of Bahloul, sharp-witted, astute and as at ease in society as he is in bed, as a model for the man of quality and the no less ambiguous figure of Badr al-Budour, beautiful and apparently virtuous yet possessed of a lascivious carnality, as an example of his female counterpart. These are the best in the book; the others fail to rise above the merely illustrative, however picaresque.

In these stories, we are well and truly in the realms of fantasy. Strong but unstated socio-religious constraints contrast sharply with the uninhibited and outrageously exaggerated behaviour of the characters. It is from the details of this contrast that the humour for al-Nafzawi's audience springs but, needing explanation, the humour may lack the same appeal for readers unfamiliar with the Arabo-Muslim cultural background. The story of Musaylima and Sajah in Chapter One is a case in point where, in the poem he recites to her, the rascal is proposing intercourse in a series of positions that correspond to those of ritual prayer.

Al-Nafzawi addresses *The Perfumed Garden* to his sponsor, the Minister, but the intended readership would appear to be a wider audience of contemporaries uneducated in matters of sex. The stories, jokes and poems are written in a simple, populist style and designed to break the ice for just this kind of sensitive and unlearned audience. The lists of members' names in Chapters Eight and Nine, for example, while supposed to be illustrative, are clearly intended to amuse as well.

With few exceptions, these stories, anecdotes and jokes have one moral in common, which brings us to the purpose of the book's composition. They illustrate, more or less colourfully, that a wife will inevitably be unfaithful to the husband who neglects her sexually or whose sexual performance is not up to the mark. It is sex that holds a marriage together and a husband's responsibility to ensure that his wife is sexually content. While polygamy may have been legitimate under Islamic law, it was never the reality for the majority of men. With this little book, al-Nafzawi offers a prescription to prevent marital breakdown on sexual grounds. The tales illustrate the problem, while the medical and nutritional sections, along with those on bedroom behaviour, suggest the cure. Seen in this light, *The Perfumed Garden* does indeed, as its author claims, have a rather honourable purpose. The Minister anticipates the sort of reaction the book might receive when he remarks that "only an idiot or half-educated fool would laugh at this or shut his eyes to it". Poignant comment in the light of its treatment over the last century.

*

The book has suffered harshly from European misinterpretation and elaboration of its content. The first translation of *The Perfumed Garden* into a European language was a French version made around 1850 by the discreetly-named Baron R..., of which thirty-five lithographed copies were produced in 1876. Despite errors and additions, this formed the basis for all subsequently published editions and translations into other European languages, errors and additions compounded, until a new French translation appeared in 1976.[6] The well-known English version by Sir Richard Burton was translated from the French of 1876.[7] In Burton's version, details were expanded, episodes introduced and whole sections incorporated from other, non-Arabic, sources. The text is dressed up in a florid prose alien to the style of the original and many of the notes are sheer speculation. The result is a consistently exaggerated and bizarre misrepresentation of the original (the 1963 edition preserves all of this while omitting – on grounds of taste – some elements that do appear in the original). Other, short-lived English versions, appearing at various times in Paris, similarly derive from the first French version. A second English translation that Burton claimed to have completed from an Arabic original, shortly before his death in 1890, was subsequently destroyed by his widow. The provenance of the exotic Carrington version is obscure. The

---

[6] R. Khawam (trans.), *La prairie parfumée où s'ébattent les plaisirs*, (Paris, Phébus: 1976). The Arabic text from which this translation was made has not been published.
[7] This edition was reprinted in 1995 (London, HarperCollins).

present translation, then, is the first from Arabic into English to be published. More to the point, it is the only one based upon an established, reliable text: Abu 'Abdullah Muhammad ibn Muhammad al-Nafzawi, *ar-rawd al-'âtir fi nuzhati'l khâtir*, ed. J. Juma'a (London, Riyad El-Rayyes: 1990).[8] That the translation is substantially shorter than Burton's version is accounted for by the absence of foreign and fanciful material.

The poems with which al-Nafzawi spices his book have some piquancy but are hard to describe as quality verse (even if one or two are reminiscent of John Wilmot). Many suggest nothing so much as limericks. This suits the author's purpose and, where appropriate, is how I have chosen to translate them. A few have been reduced in length. Formulaic religious expressions have been reduced in number and the formal address to al-Nafzawi's sponsor with which every chapter in the original begins has been retained only in Chapter One. Several other repetitions have also been removed. The text is otherwise complete, although, for example, the interpretation of dreams which rely on lexical analysis of Arabic words can have little, if any, meaning for the non-Arabic speaking dreamer; these have been set in a lower font.

I am confident of having identified most of the plants, spices, etc. mentioned in the text, on the basis of available sources.[9] Where the translation offers, for example, "mixed spice" as an ingredient of some aphrodisiac concoction, this is not an obfuscation on my part but what the author wrote. He is also rather vague on weights and measures. The title could be translated rather more literally but I have preferred to remain with the one by which the book has come to be known in English, only translating it fully as *The Perfumed Garden of Sensual Delight*. The transliteration of Arabic words in the body of the text approximates to the Library of Congress system, minus diacritical marks.

---

[8] The only other published edition of which I am aware is: Sheikh Sidi Muhammad ibn Muhammad al-Nafzawi, *ar-rawd al-'âtir fi nuzhati'l khâtir*, (Tunis: *s.d.*); no use has been made of this in the present translation.
[9] These sources are: Avicenna, *al-qânûn fi-ttib* [The Canon of Medicine], 4 vols., eds. E. Qash & A. Zayour, (Beirut: 1993); F. Kanz, *al-a'shâb at-tibbîya* [Medicinal Plants], (Sousse, Tunisia: 1994); E. M. Chéhabi, *Dictionnaire des Termes Agricoles* (Beirut: 1957). Several shopkeepers in *souq al-belat* – the medicinal herb market – of the Tunis *medina* helped me to identify some of the more obscure items.

Al-Nafzawi's writing carries a marked North African imprint. In writing for the common man to read (or be read to), he slips in dialect expressions and standard Arabic words with localised meanings. I would like to note my thanks to two Tunisian friends, Faysal Essmii and Fatat 'Adhra, for their help in pinning these down. The shortcomings of the translation are, of course, mine alone.

The Perfumed Garden is a short book and short books do not need long introductions, so I will conclude with the hope that the reader of this translation will agree that it is the book of integrity its author claims and, at the same time, is not without some entertainment value. If ever a book needed demystification, it is *The Perfumed Garden*, which has no pretension to being other than the short, immodest guide for the ordinary, married man of its time that its author claims.

Jim Colville
Sidi Bou Saïd, Tunisia
April, 1997

THE PERFUMED GARDEN
OF SENSUAL DELIGHT

Preface

In the Name of God the Merciful and Compassionate.
May He bless our Lord and Master, Muhammad,
his family and descendants.

Praise be to God who has made a man and woman's supreme delight the sex of one another. Neither sex finds satisfaction and fulfilment until the man's has penetrated the woman's. And when the two connect, they lock together in a wild and savage struggle in which each one drives relentlessly towards the single climax of desire. The man will rock and the woman roll[1] until their passion is spent.

The delight of kissing a woman on her lips, cheeks and neck, of hugging and holding her tight to his breast, are ways that God has made to bring a man to arousal. In His mercy, He created woman with breasts, neck and throat, and soft, blushed cheeks. He gave her eyes to entice and eyelashes long and sharp, like shining daggers. Her belly He curved and jewelled with a navel. He made her waist and hips and firm, round buttocks and below, between her thighs, created a fabulous thing like a lion's head; and its name is cunt. To it He gave a mouth, a tongue and lips, and shape like the footprint of an ibex in the sand. How many heroes have fallen as its casualties in anguish and in sorrow! In His power and wisdom, He set all this on two wonderful limbs, not too long and not too short, gracing each with knee and calf and foot, and an ankle perfect to adorn with chains of gold and silver.

I praise the One who bathed woman in the sea of allure, delight and beauty, who made her body perfect joy to touch and hold, and her smile such sweet enchantment. I praise Him, the Omnipotent, who created woman to arouse and captivate with her finely curved figure, her breasts, her neck and hair, and so made her man's bewitching. I praise Him, the All-Powerful, who humbled man to love of her, to rest and to repose with her, who made her the cause of his committment and farewell, the motive for his settling and the reason for his flight. I praise the One who breaks and humbles lovers' hearts at parting, who burns them in the fire of un-

---

[1] Quite literally, "rock and roll"!

3

fulfilled desire and degrades them to contempt, disgrace and misery in their longing to be joined. I praise Him as His slave who can but love and take his pleasure from the love of women, powerless to relinquish or forsake them. I witness now, as I will at the hour of my death, that there is no god but God and our Lord and Master, Muhammad, is the Messenger of His Word. May God bless him, his family, descendants and companions. And may my witness avail me at the terror of His judgement.

*

This is a book of honourable purpose, written at the request of Muhammad ibn 'Awana Zawawi, Chief Minister to the Sultan of Tunis, His Excellency 'Abdal'aziz Hafsi, after he had read my previous short work, *Enlightened Performance in the Secrets of Coitus*. The Sultan's poet, adviser, secretary, confidant and friend, and an intelligent, understanding and wise man, the most worldly-wise of his day, he grew up in Algiers where he came to the Sultan's attention after the fall of that city. He removed with him to Tunis and was there appointed his Chief Minister.

When my above book came to his notice, he sent for me and insisted that I come as quickly as I could; I was received most cordially at his residence. After three days of gracious hospitality, he granted me an audience, produced my book and inquired if I really was the author.

"Do not be modest," he told me. "Everything you have written is true and no-one can take issue with it. You may not be the first to have dealt with this subject but, God knows, it's one that needs to be more widely understood. Only an idiot or half-educated fool would laugh at this or shut his eyes to it."

He then raised a number of points, suggesting that I expand some chapters and incorporate additional ones. In particular, he suggested the sections on the various remedies, which had been dealt with only briefly, should be expanded, unabridged versions of stories should be given, and the causes of sexual desire and reasons for abstinence should be explained. Methods of treating erection problems, of penis enlargement, of removing vaginal odour and of tightening the vagina, and treatments relating to pregnancy, should be also be included. In this way, he suggested, my book would become more comprehensive and achieve its aim more readily. I assured him that this would not be difficult to do. And so, seeking help from God and with prayers to the Messenger of His Word, I set about composing this book which I have called *The Perfumed Garden of Sensual Delight*. Success is God's alone to grant or withhold and His alone is the power and the glory.

The book is arranged in chapters – twenty-one in all – to enable the reader more easily to find the topic he requires. Where appropriate, I have included tried and tested advice and remedies, as well as tales and anecdotes of cunning and intrigue. The arrangement is as follows:

Chapter One

The Man of Quality

You will be aware, Your Excellency – and may God be merciful to you – that there are many different types of men and women; among them are those who have quality and among them are those who do not.

For a woman, the man of quality has a large, hard and vigorous penis, quick to rise in the ache of its desire and slow to spend its passion. For intercourse, a woman enjoys a man who gives and takes his pleasure slowly, with gentle breast and heavy haunches, a man of size whose penis reaches deep within her vagina, to stretch her and to fill her, a man who is slow to come and quick to arousal again. Such a man is a woman's pleasure. A poet said,

> *Women desire what in men cannot last,*
> *Youth, wealth and health, and not coming too fast,*
> *Long-lasting and slow is what women expect*
> *And for seconds, he's equally quick to erect.*
> *Well-endowed, heavy-haunched with a light, gentle breast,*
> *The man who has these, among women, is blessed.*

There is a story that one day the Caliph 'Abdulmalik ibn Marwan[2] met the poetess Layla Akhiliya and put all sorts of questions to her. They then had the following exchange:

"Layla, what is it in a man that women cherish?"

"Cheeks like a woman's, Sire," she replied.

"What else?"

"Hair like a woman's."

"And what else?"

"Sire, an older man needs authority or wealth to find success with women – so a man just like you, Commander of the Faithful."

A poet composed the following verses about this:

---

[2] 'Abdulmalik ibn Marwan: the fifth Umayyad Caliph (685-705).

Women to riches and wealth are in thrall,
A young man with land is, for them, best of all.
When a man's hair turns grey or his fortune grows less,
He will find himself lacking a woman's caress.

*

The width of twelve fingers, or three hands, is the length of the largest male members, while the smallest are the length of six fingers-width, or one and one half hands. Some men measure twelve and some men ten, or two and one half hands, while some measure eight and others six. Anything less is no use to a woman.

*

One of the stimulants to sexual desire is the use of perfume by both partners. When a woman detects the scent of perfume on a man, she relaxes and unwinds. A man might thus try perfume as a means to coupling with a woman.

With this is mind, let us relate a story about Musaylima ibn Qays – may God curse him – the liar who claimed prophecy in the time of the true Prophet – may God bless him – and a band of perfidious Bedouin – may God damn them all!

This Musaylima used to produce his own fake and distorted versions of Quranic verses. A gang of hypocrites and dissenters once brought him the chapter of the Quran entitled, 'The Elephant', revealed to the Prophet Muhammad by the angel Gabriel.

"Gabriel revealed one just like it to me!" he announced and proceeded to recite,

"The elephant, who told you about the elephant? It has a tail like a rope and a very long nose. It is one of God's creatures" (*sic!*).

He also produced a fake version of the chapter entitled, 'al-Kawthar'[3] that went:

"We have given you jewels, so choose what you will. But be quick about it and do not be greedy!" He distorted other chapters in a similarly facile way.

---

[3] 'The Elephant' (*al-Fil*): Quran, chapter 105; *al-Kawthar* is chapter 108.

7

Some of Musaylima's tribe had seen or heard that when Muhammad placed his hand on the head of a bald man, the hair grew back, or if he spat in a dried-up well, it filled with fresh water. If he spat in the eye of a blind man or of someone suffering from ophthalmia, the sight would be restored, while if he placed his hand on a child's head and said, "May he live for one hundred years!" the child would live to be a hundred.

"Have you seen what Muhammad can do?" they asked him.

"I can do better than that," was Musaylima's reply.

But in trying to imitate the Prophet, this enemy of God would place his hand on the head of a balding man and what little hair he had fell out. If he spat in a well, the water either dried up or turned salty and by spitting in the eye of someone suffering from ophthalmia, he became permanently blind there and then. When he laid his hand on a child's head and said, "Live for a hundred years!" the child immediately dropped down dead.

Just look, my friends, at what the scoundrel got up to! Success is in God's hands alone to grant or to withhold.

Now, in those days, there was a woman by the name of Sajah, from the tribe of Banu Tamim, who also claimed prophecy. Both she and Musaylima had heard of each other. Once, some time after the death of the Prophet Muhammad, she announced to a full war party of her tribe,

"Prophets do not come in pairs. Either he is a prophet and we shall all follow him or I am one and he and his tribe shall follow me."

So she sent him a message, of which the content was:

"Prophecy does not coincide in two people at one time. Let us meet among a gathering of our two tribes and together examine what we have received in the way of revelation. Whoever speaks the truth shall be the one to follow."

She sealed it and told the messenger,

"Take this letter to the Yamama and give it to Musaylima ibn Qays. I will follow later with the army."

The next day, she and her tribe broke camp.

When he opened the letter and read its contents, Musaylima grew alarmed. He asked each member of his tribe for advice on what to do but no-one could give him a satisfactory answer. He was in a state of some anxiety when an old man came up to him.

"Calm down, Musaylima, relax! I'm going to give you a little fatherly advice."

8

"Let's have it then. I need all the advice I can get."

"Tomorrow morning, pitch a vaulted tent of coloured brocade just outside the camp. Spread silks and sprinkle perfumed waters – lily, rose, carnation, violet and the like. Fill censers with Khymer aloes, ambergris and musk and perfume the interior. Loosen the tent ropes so none of the incense escapes and once the damp canvas has absorbed the smoke, take your seat and send for her. Invite her to join you alone in the tent. Once inside, the scent of the incense and perfume will relax and unwind her and she'll begin to lose control. At that point, take advantage of her and she will do whatever you want. Screw her and rid yourself of the wickedness of her and her tribe."

"Well spoken," said a reassured Musaylima. "That's the best advice I've had."

He did exactly as the old man had suggested and when Sajah arrived, invited her into the tent for private discussions. Sure enough, as they talked, she became steadily more and more confused. Aware that her distraction was sexual, he recited this poem to her:

The bedroom's prepared, pray let us go through,
Lie down on your back, I'll show something to you,
Take it bending or squatting, on your hands and your knees,
Take two-thirds or all of it, whatever would please!

"All of it! Yes, all of it!" she cried. "Show me everything, you prophet!"

So he jumped on top of her and had his way.

"When I've gone, ask my people for my hand in marriage," she said afterwards.

She left him later and returned to her tribe.

"What do you think?" they asked.

"Well, he revealed his prophethood to me and I found him upright and upstanding, so I submitted to him!"

Her people consented to give her to Musaylima in marriage and in response to their demand for a dowry, he told them they need not observe the afternoon prayer. To this day, the tribe of Tamim do not observe that prayer, claiming that, as the dowry of their prophetess, it is their exclusive right. She was the only woman ever to have claimed prophecy and about her, one of the poets of Tamim composed these lines:

Our prophet was a woman, around her we trod,
While men one and all were the prophets of God.

Musaylima was eventually killed during the reign of the first Caliph, Abu Bakr Siddiq. Opinions differ as to who killed him. Some say it was Zayd ibn al-Khattab while others claim it was Wahshi, another of the Prophet's Companions. I believe it was Wahshi, on the basis of his statement that he "killed the best of men in the time of ignorance before Islam, Hamza ibn 'Abdalmuttalib,[4] and the worst after the coming of Islam, Musaylima. May God forgive me the former by virtue of the latter." As for Sajah, she saw the error of her ways and repented, accepting Islam and marrying one of the Prophet's companions.

*

The man of quality should be purposeful and serious, clean and well-groomed, of good build and handsome appearance. He should always speak the truth and never lie. He should be courageous and generous, with a noble spirit and a gentle heart. He will do what he says and never betray a confidence or break a promise. That is the sort of man women will cherish and desire to be loved and be fucked by. The repulsive man is discussed in the next chapter.

*

During the reign of the Caliph Ma'moun,[5] there lived a character by the name of Bahloul who was something of a jester and a frequent butt of jokes by the royal family and courtiers. One day, so the story goes, no sooner had he entered the court and been invited to sit down, than the Caliph slapped him across the back of the head.

"What brings you here, you son of a whore?" he laughed.

"I've come to see my master, may God send him victorious," replied Bahloul.

---

[4] Hamza ibn 'Abdalmuttalib: the uncle of the Prophet.

[5] Ma'moun ibn Haroun: the seventh Abbasid Caliph (812-833).

"How are you getting on with your two women?" asked the Caliph, aware that Bahloul had recently taken a second wife.

"Sire, I'm powerless to control the new one, the old one's a law unto herself and I'm staring poverty in the face."

"If you can put that into verse, Bahloul, we're listening," said the Caliph.

So Bahloul recited,

Poverty holds me in its chains, it tortures and torments,
God has forsaken such as me and mankind shows contempt.
If my poverty continues, without change to my position,
Then I will be, quite certainly, homeless and in perdition.

"And where would you go?" asked the Caliph.

"To God, His Messenger, and to you, Commander of the Faithful."

"Well said! Whoever seeks refuge in God and His Messenger – and us – we welcome. Now, have you perhaps given expression to your marital predicament in verse, too, Bahloul?"

"I have indeed, Sire."

"Come on then, let's hear it!"

So Bahloul recited this poem:

I've taken two wives, poor fool that I am,
I thought I'd be pampered in bed like a lamb,
Lying in clover 'twixt two pairs of breasts
But instead I find nightly I'm put to the test
By two ravenous wolves who take nights in turn
And in giving one pleasure, the other's rage burns.

Each night there is constant abuse and derision,
One woman's enough for two whole divisions!
So take my advice for an honourable life
And live as a bachelor, without trouble and strife
But if that is something that cannot be done
Then from that awful regiment, take only one!

This sent the Caliph into a fit of laughter and he rewarded Bahloul with the gift of a very fine, golden tunic. And so, in much better spirits than when he had arrived, Bahloul made his exit.

On his way home, he passed by the residence of the Grand Vizier where Hamdouna, the Caliph's sister and wife of the Vizier, was at home in her observatory. She happened to look down and see him.

"There's Bahloul, and wearing a golden tunic," she remarked to her maid. "Now, how can I take that off him?"

"You won't be able to, Madam."

"I can outsmart that one."

"Bahloul's a shrewd man, Madam. People think they're laughing at him but really he's the one who's laughing. Leave him alone or he'll drop you in the pit that you would dig for him."

"I want that tunic!" Hamdouna insisted and sent the maid to fetch him.

"My mistress invites you inside," she said.

"One should always accept an invitation," Bahloul replied and followed her into the palace.

"I think you've come to listen to my singing, haven't you, Bahloul?" Hamdouna said. In fact, she was a very fine singer.

"That's right, Madam."

"And afterwards, you'd like a little refreshment, would you not?"

"I would indeed, Madam," he agreed.

So she sang to him in a quite lovely voice and afterwards had food and drink brought. Then she continued,

"Bahloul, I do believe you'd like to take off that fine tunic you have on and give it to me, wouldn't you?"

"There is one condition, Madam. I made a promise to myself I'd only give it to the woman who lets me do with her what a man does with his wife."

"And what would you know about that, Bahloul?"

"Ha! God gave me all the talents to please! I know all there is to know about the needs and wants of women. There's no man more skilful than me!"

Now, Hamdouna was a very beautiful woman, the most attractive of her day. Otherwise brave men who saw her were humbled and lowered their gaze for fear of her God-given, sirene-like charms. Any man who dared look into her eyes was bewitched and many were the heroes she had ruined. She had, in the past, sent notes to Bahloul but he had always turned her down, afraid that he, too, would end up bewitched by this *femme fatale*. And there the matter had remained – until that day, that is.

They settle into conversation. Sometimes he looks straight at her and sometimes his eyes do not leave the ground. Whenever she tries to tempt him into parting with the tunic, he teases her by talk of how much it will cost.

"Which is?" she wants to know.

"Intimacy, Madam!" he replies.

"And what would you know about that?"

"The lot! Women are my speciality. No-one takes the care that I do on the job. In affairs of this world, Madam, men's motives and desires are very different. Some men give and some men take, some men buy and some men sell. Not me. All that interests me is making love, attending to the needs of pussies in distress and satisfying women's thirst."

This kind of talk rather appealed to her.

"If you've written any verses about that, Bahloul, I would like to hear them," says she.

So Bahloul recites:

Mankind may differ in wealth and in fame,
In conduct and custom and deeds they have done,
Some enjoy good name while others know shame,
There are some who have fortune and those who have none.

But I care not for things by which others are led,
Be they Arab or Turkish or Persian –
Only women in bed, whether virgin or wed
And the wonderful act of coition!

To your honour and rank I accord the respect
Of a slave, humble in front of his mistress
But I did not expect that you would reject
My proposal of passionate congress.

As a lover, no woman has known me to tire,
Of that you may have heard mention,

13

Is it not your desire that I cool down your fire
With this member of splendid dimension?

You will marvel indeed at its vigour and lust,
To self-doubt, it pays no attention;
By quenching your thirst, when I mount you and thrust,
You will know it has just one intention.

Now let me caress you, reject me no more,
Don't deny he who loves you your love,
If once only should bore you, why then I implore you
To fuck me 'til you've had enough!

So lie down beside me, attend to my prick,
It suffers the pain of rejection.
I play you no trick, for it is truly sick –
Be a nursemaid and treat my erection!

And there's no need to fear for your virtuous name,
Of what people would say if they knew.
You will not be blamed, disgraced, scorned or shamed,
Since no-one will know but we two!

Listening to this, Hamdouna begins to relax and can't stop herself glancing at Bahloul's erection, straight as a flagpole, in front of her. She doesn't know what to do but soon the lust rising warm between her legs takes control. The Devil makes her blood hot and the thought of bedding him excites her.

"If he does it to me and shouts his mouth off afterwards, no-one will ever believe him," she reasons.

"Take off the tunic and come up to my bedroom, Bahloul."

"It's yours once I get what I want, darling!"

Aching and shaking with lust for him, she rises and makes her way upstairs, undoing her belt as she goes.

"Am I dreaming," wonders Bahloul, as he follows, "or is this for real?"

Entering the bedroom, she lies down upon the silk sheets of her bed. With her skirt above her thighs and her God-given loveliness on full display, she begins to caress herself in front of him. He gazes at her belly's gentle swell and the broadness of her navel, drawing breath upon her naked thighs and the marvellous thing between them, fluttering like a flag does in a gentle breeze. He goes down on her and kisses her repeatedly. She slips into a swoon and starts to stroke him up and down, hardly aware of what she's doing.

"Madam, what a state you're in!"

"You son of a bitch!" she moans. "I was like a mare on heat before and now you've made it quite unbearable. Your kind of talk could undo a saint. Your words are lethal!"

"But you're a married woman, so how come you're so hot?"

"What has married got to do with it? Some women get turned on by talk and others, if they've not done it for a while, can get turned on by any man – like a mare does by a stallion. Talk turns me on *and* I've not been speaking to my husband. So get on with it because he usually comes home about now!"

"My back hurts and I can't mount you. Why don't you get on top and do it? Then you can have the tunic and let me be on my way."

Bahloul lies down on his back, as a woman would do for a man, his penis upright like a flagpole. Hamdouna sits astride him and takes a hold of it. She admires it, amazed – and delighted – by its splendid size.

"This is a woman's ruin," she gasps. "I've *never* seen one as big as yours, Bahloul!"

She holds him against herself, easing it into her then slides down onto him and the whole thing vanishes inside her.

"God damn women!" laughs Bahloul. "They're always losing things!"

She starts bouncing up and down, stirring it around and squeezing him inside her, until the two of them climax together. She takes hold of it again and eases herself off him, slowly.

"This is a man!" she sighs, gazing at it.

She wipes it for him then he gets up and makes to leave.

"And where's the tunic?"

"Madam, you've just fucked me. What more do you want?"

"You told me your back hurt and that you couldn't do it."

"I never thought you'd do it to me. Now you owe me one and it will be my turn to do it. That's what the tunic costs and then you can discharge me."

"Well, I've come this far," she thinks as she cuddles up to him again. "He'll go once we've done it a second time."

"I'll only do it if you undress completely," he tells her.

Hamdouna takes off all her clothes and Bahloul can only marvel at the beauty of her fully naked body. From top to bottom, he explores every part of her, before again arriving at that place.

"Ah! This is a man's enslavement," he whispers as he licks and kisses it over and over until her climax comes close.

She takes hold of him, guides him inside her and they begin to rock and roll until, eventually, they come.

"Off with the tunic!" she shouts as he's about to leave.

"But that's us all square now."

"Are you making fun of me?"

"The tunic is yours when you've paid for it," he insists.

"How much?" she demands, glaring at him.

"You had the first one and I got the second, so that makes us equal. A third time and it's paid for," he tells her, taking off the tunic, folding it and placing it in front of her.

"Do what you want!" she sighs, opening her legs once more.

He mounts her and slips it inside while she, pushing hard against him, matches all his movements until they come together. Then he gets up and goes, leaving the tunic behind him.

"Didn't I tell you that Bahloul's a sharp character," said the maid, "and that you wouldn't get the better of him? But did you believe me?"

"Shut up!" snapped Hamdouna. "What happened, happened. Every pussy has it's lover's name upon it, for better or for worse. If mine had not had Bahloul's on it, he would not have had me with a present of the world and everything within it."

Suddenly there was a knock upon the door.

"Who's there?" asked the maid

"Bahloul," came the reply.

The Vizier's wife was surprised to hear his voice.

"What do you want?" asked the maid.

"A drink of water!"

The maid took him out a jug of water but after he had drunk, Bahloul let the jug drop on the ground and smash. The maid slammed the door and left him sitting there. Presently, the Vizier came home.

"What are you doing here, Bahloul?"

"Sir, I was passing and got taken thirsty so I knocked on the door and the maid brought me a jug of water but it slipped from my hands and broke and, by way of compensation, Madam Hamdouna took the tunic that our master, the Commander of the Faithful, had given me."

"Bring the tunic here!" ordered the Vizier.

Hamdouna appeared at the door.

"Did you make Bahloul pay for a broken jug with that priceless tunic?"

"Is that how it was, Bahloul?" she asked, clasping her hands.

"I've explained what happened in my artless way, Madam, now you tell it with finesse!"

Speechless, she handed him the tunic, which he slipped on and went upon his way.

Chapter Two

The Woman of Quality

There are many different types of women, some of whom are attractive and desirable to men and some of whom are not. For a man, the woman of quality has a full and voluptuous figure, jet-black hair, a broad forehead, arched eyebrows and wide, clear eyes, a moon-shaped face, smooth, soft cheeks, a straight nose and narrow mouth, sweet breath, red lips and a pink tongue. She has a long neck and full throat, broad shoulders and chest with large, firm breasts and a deep cleavage, a neat waist and curved belly with a wide, deep navel, a generous vulva, a soft, tight vagina without discharge or odour – and hot, as if almost on fire – broad hips, firm, ample buttocks, tight curves, firm, strong thighs, long, shapely legs, graceful feet, broad arms and elegant hands. As she walks towards you, she entrances and when she turns around, she's fatal. When she sits, her vulva pouts like a little cupola; lying down, it flutters like a flag does in a gentle breeze and when she stands, it stands majestic like a sceptre.

She will not be given to much laughter or frivolous talk nor to much coming and going to the houses of neighbours (with whom she will, in any case, have few dealings). She will not seek the close friendship of other women but will be at ease with and put her trust in her husband alone. She will eat only at his table or at that of close relatives, if she has any. She will not behave secretively towards her husband, nor betray a confidence, nor will she deceive him. If her husband calls her to bed, she will obey him by preceding him. She will help him in all manner of things. She will complain little, neither will she cause offence. She will relax and laugh only in the intimacy of her husband's company and will give herself to him alone, even though she were to die of forbearance.

*

There is a story, of doubtful provenance, about a great and power-ful king a very long time ago, called 'Ali ibn Daygham who, one night, was suffering from an impossible case of insomnia. He called for his

Vizier, Chief of Police and Commander of the Guard and ordered them to fasten their swords.

"What's the matter?" they inquired.

"I cannot sleep tonight," he said, "and want to make a round of the city. You three will accompany me."

"We hear and we obey."

"In the Name of God and with the blessings of His Messenger," intoned the King, as off he went with his retinue in tow.

Around the town from street to street they went until, suddenly, they heard a noise coming from down an alleyway. There, they found a drunk man rolling in the dust and beating his chest with a stone.

"Justice is lost," he was crying. "It's dead and buried and black are the hearts of men! No-one will tell the King what's happening in his own kingdom."

"Bring him here," ordered the King, "but be careful not to alarm him."

"Stand up and do not be afraid, no harm will come to you," they said as they approached the man and took him by the arm.

"How can you tell me not to be afraid and that no harm will come to me when you don't even greet me with 'Peace upon you'? It guarantees safety, you know, and a Muslim suspects treachery if another does not greet him with those words."

Nevertheless, up he got and was brought before the King, who sat with his face covered. His retinue, likewise, had their faces covered as they stood around him, leaning on their swords.

"Peace upon you, whoever you are," the man addressed the King.

"And peace upon you, too, whoever you are," the King replied.

"Why do you address me as 'whoever you are'?"

"I could ask the same question."

"I don't know your name."

"Neither do I know yours but just now I heard you shouting that there is no justice any more and no-one will tell the King what is happening in his kingdom. Tell me what has happened to you."

"I'll only tell the man who will avenge me and bring disgrace and shame to light."

"God willing, that is what I will do."

"Well, my story's a strange one and my predicament is queer," began the man. "I was as in love with a woman as she was with me and we had been carrying on a long-term affair. However, an old hag led her astray and took her to a house of debauchery, depravity and lust. Now sleep has forsaken me, my happiness has gone and I live a life of unremitting misery."

"Where is this brothel and who's got your woman?" asked the King.

"A black slave by the name of Dirgham has her. He has other women there, too, all lovely like moons, more beautiful even than the King's harem."

"To whom does he belong?"

"He's a runaway belonging to the Grand Vizier. He has a mistress who's infatuated with him and brings him food, drink and clothes and anything else he needs."

The King listened to all of this with amazement, as did the Vizier, who recognised the slave as his own.

"Show me where this house is," the King demanded.

"And if I take you there, what will you do?"

"Just wait and see."

"Not a lot, I think," the drunk man opined. "It's a grim, imposing building and Dirgham is a vicious, violent man. Using force will only put your life at risk."

"Just show me where it is and leave the worrying to me."

"God help us!"

So off they go with the drunk leading the way, until they come to a wide alley and a house behind a massive door and towering walls. Seeing no way in, they gaze at it in dismay. Then the King turned to the drunk man and asked him his name.

"'Umar ibn Sa'd."

"Are you strong, 'Umar?"

"I am indeed."

"Can any of you scale this wall?" he asked, turning to his retinue.

"No way!" they replied with one voice.

"Then I will – but with a little cunning and your help."

"What do you mean?"

"Tell me, which of you is the strongest?"

"The Chief of Police, he's the Executioner."

"And after him?"

"The Commander of the Guard."

20

"Then?"

"The Grand Vizier."

"And next?"

'Umar listened in amazement to all of this. Realising to whom he had been speaking, he was transported with excitement.

"Me, Your Majesty! Me!"

"'Umar," said the King, "we have taken you into our confidence and now you know who we are. No harm will come to you if you keep our secret safe."

The King then told the Executioner,

"Lean your hands against the wall and keep your feet apart."

The Commander of the Guard was ordered,

"Climb onto his back, put your feet on his shoulders and lean your hands against the wall."

The Vizier was told to do the same.

"Now, 'Umar, you climb up on top."

'Umar was astonished at this arrangement.

"God bless you, Sire, and your most apposite presence of mind."

One by one, he climbed over the backs of the Executioner, the Commander of the Guard and the Vizier until he stood with his feet on the latter's shoulders. Only the King was left.

"Keep still and I will reward you well," he told each man as he climbed over his back, telling 'Umar,

"I have made you my confidant. Hold steady and keep still!"

Standing upon his shoulders, he took hold of the edge of the roof and, with a murmured prayer, pulled himself clean up in one.

"Now get down, one by one," he said.

This they did, much impressed by the King's ingenuity and the sheer strength of the Executioner in taking the weight of four armed men.

The King meanwhile looked for a way down to the other side. Finding none, he unrolled his turban, looped it around a window grille and lowered himself down to the courtyard below. As he explored his surroundings, he came to the door to the outside, bolted with an enormous lock. His heart sank.

"By the Grace of God I've got this far but I'll never get out the same way," he thought.

Carrying on around the courtyard, he counted the rooms. which he estimated at seventeen. The courtyard itself was covered from wall to wall with golden carpets and rugs of coloured silk. Suddenly, he became aware of the sound of voices coming from a room at the top of seven flights of stairs. He made for the foot of the stairs.

"Lord, bring me home safely!" he muttered as he climbed the first flight. The steps, he noticed, were of variegated marble, dappled in many colours. "With God's help, no-one can harm you," he reassured himself, beginning upon the second flight. "Lord, I place my trust in You," he said, creeping up the third. "God help me!" he whispered as he tiptoed up the fourth. And so on he continued up the fifth, sixth and seventh flights of stairs until he came to a doorway with a red silk curtain hung across it.

He gazed inside at a room brightly lit with candles burning in golden chandeliers. In the middle was a gushing fountain and a table laid from end to end with fruit and all kinds of good things to eat. Golden carpets were piled thickly on the floor and so bright that even dazzled eyes would see them. And around the table, sat twelve girls and seven women, all radiantly beautiful like shining moons, carousing with seven slaves. Bottles of wine lay on the table before them and everyone was in party mood. They had all clearly had their fill of wine. Suddenly, a young woman caught his eye, a stunning, graceful, dark-eyed, soft-skinned woman with a figure to capture the heart and a perfect beauty he could not describe.

"Get a grip of yourself and concentrate on getting out of here!" he told himself.

While thus meditating on his own deliverance, he overheard one of the women say to two of her friends,

"Come on, darlings, it's late and we're tired. Let's take a light through to the bedroom and lie down."

The three of them stood up, went through to a bedroom and lit the lamp. When they came out again to pay a call of nature, the King crept into their room and hid behind a screen. His thoughts went out to his men back in the alley, who were themselves anxious that their King's life was in danger.

The women returned the worse for drink and shut the door behind them. They took off all their clothes and started to make love.

"'Umar could not have been more right," gasped the King, "when he described this place as a den of depravity and pit of debauchery!"

As the three women began to drift asleep, the King rose and put out the light, took off his clothes and slipped into bed beside them.

"Where are the keys, sweetheart?" he whispered to one of them.

"They're where they always are," she replied. "Go to sleep."

"Good God, this will not be easy," he thought.

"Where have you put the keys, dear?" he whispered to another. "It'll be morning soon and when it's light I have to open the doors and sweep the courtyard."

"The keys are where they always are," she answered wearily, "and it's not your job to do the cleaning. Go to sleep!"

"I'd run them through with my sword, were it not for fear of God," he thought.

"Darling?" he whispered to the third.

"What is it?" She had a deep voice.

"I can't remember where the keys are. Tell me where you put them."

"You slut, may your cunt itch and your climax stall! You can't do without it for a single night and there's the Vizier's daughter-in-law who's rejected all of Dirgham's advances every night for the last six months. The keys are in the slave's pocket but you needn't bother asking for them, just say 'Give me your dick, Dirgham!' Now leave me alone!"

She fell silent then and the King said nothing more. He knew what had to be done. He waited until he was certain she had fallen asleep and then slipped quietly out of bed. He picked up her clothes and put them on, fastening his sword underneath and covering his face with a red silk veil. Dressed so, he might pass for a woman. He opened the door carefully and crept towards the dining room. Stopping behind the curtain, he peeped inside and saw that the entire company were much the worse for drink. Some lay sprawled out, although others could still sit up.

"Your kingdom ends at this threshold," he told himself. "You're about to fall among a gang of drunks who could not tell the King from one of his subjects. Now show yourself!"

With a silent prayer, he made his entrance. Pretending to be drunk, he staggered towards a divan. Dirgham and the others thought that he was one of the three women who had left earlier. Watching her collapse on top of the divan, Dirgham supposed she had returned for sex and this gave him the hots.

"Get your kit off, sweetheart," he leered, "and get under the covers until I'm ready for you."

"Oh, my God, 'Umar was right!"

He looked around the room, groped in drawers and pockets but found no keys anywhere.

"Oh well, what God wills, will be," he sighed, raising his eyes to the heavens.

And there, hanging from a skylight, he spotted a gold-embroidered tunic. Reaching up, he put his hand into the pocket and brought out seven keys, the right number for all the doors.

"Praise the Lord! Now to charm my way out of here."

He stood up and, retching as if about to vomit, staggered into the middle of the room.

"God bless you, darling!" Dirgham sneered. "Anyone else would have thrown up on the bed."

The King made the first door, opened it, locked it behind him then the second, the third and so on until, beyond the seventh door, he found himself standing in front of his astonished companions who showered him with questions.

"Now is not the time to explain. It will soon be light, so let's get a move on! But watch how you go. There are seven slaves in there with twelve girls and seven of the loveliest women you have ever seen!"

Highly impressed by the King's courage, they followed him inside.

"May I ask why you're wearing women's clothes, Sire?" asked the Vizier.

"Be quiet! Without these clothes I could never have found the keys."

The King crept into the bedroom, where he took off the woman's clothes and put his own back on. Then he led his men to the room where the slaves and the women were. Coming to a halt in front of the curtain, they peeped inside. They all agreed that the woman they saw sitting on a raised divan was the loveliest of them all.

"She's mine," said the King, "unless someone else has already had her."

At this point, Dirgham fell out of bed, followed by a very beautiful woman. A second slave then climbed in with another woman and so on until six of the women had been taken. Each one hopped into bed enthusiastically and tumbled out afterwards exhausted. Only the girls and that one woman, the most beautiful of all by common consent, were left. One after the other, the slaves began making passes at her but she rejected every one.

"I will never do it," she declared, "nor will these girls in my care."

Dirgham then stood up, his erection as big as a flagpole, and began slapping it about her face and head.

"For six months we've been trying to do it to you and for six months you've refused. Tonight's the night that you'll get fucked!"

Although he was drunk, she could see that he obviously meant what he said and began calming him and making all sorts of promises.

"I'm fed up with your flattery and promises," he growled.

"Sit down here and tonight you will have what you want," she said in a soothing voice.

So he sat down in front of her, still visibly very erect. The King was quite astonished. And, as if from the bottom of her heart, she sighed and sang this song:

How I long for my lover who loves me and no other,
His pleasure, my treasure, my pleasure, his measure,
His thing long and thick like a slick candlestick,
So strong, never weak, in creation, unique,
And hard, never sleeping, at my sex always weeping,
He licks me, he bites me, his caresses excite me,
He needs no assistance and finds no resistance,
He kisses and sucks me, when I'm ready he fucks me,
And parting my thighs, I feel I could die.
As he enters and thrusts, my release is his lust,
He mounts and he rides me, I squeeze him inside me,
He kneads me, he screws me, I love him to use me,
He kisses all over, makes me roll and bend over,
I scream and I shout, "Don't take your thing out!"
Then we climax as one and our passion is done.
Ah! My lover, so handsome – my soul be his ransom,
He has sworn to delight for seventy nights,
Then I'll have him beside me and once more inside me,
And his kisses so sweet will my rapture complete.

Her singing brought the King to a state of high arousal.

"God damn you, woman!" he muttered and turned around to his men.

"I'm convinced that, although she doesn't have a man, this woman is no whore."

"You're right, Sire," confirmed 'Umar. "She's been separated from her husband for almost a year now and despite plenty of propositions, she's given in to no-one."

"Who is her husband?"

"The son of your father's Vizier, Sire."

"Yes, I'd heard he had a beautiful and virtuous wife."

"That's her."

"Nevertheless, I'm going to have her. Now, where's your woman, 'Umar ?"

"I don't see her, Sire."

"Be patient and I will find her for you," said the King, whose resourcefulness was a source of undiminished wonder to 'Umar. "There's the slave, Dirgham."

"He belongs to me," said the Vizier.

"Shut up!" snapped the King. "This is not the place to talk."

Dirgham, meanwhile, was still trying to have his animal way with the woman.

"I'm tired of your lies, Badr al-Budour," he growled.

"Badr al-Budour," repeated the King. "What a lovely name!"[6]

The slave slapped her and dragged her across the room by the hair, which made the King seethe with rage and jealousy.

"Do you see what your slave is doing?" he hissed at the Vizier. "By God, he will die an awful death as a warning to others like him."

"Would you be disloyal and betray the Vizier's wife?" Badr al-Budour appealed to the slave. "Have you forgotten your affair with her and how well she treated you?"

"Did you hear that?" asked the King. The Vizier made no reply.

She then stood up and, returning to her seat, began to sing,

---

[6] Badr al-Budour, literally, "the brightest of full moons" – the moon often being used as an epithet for beauty.

Man's brow is lined deep with woman's deception,
Love constant as fortune that only betrays,
In bed she's your lover and there's the temptation,
Even brave men are fooled by the sweet things she says.

She knows no commitment, her friendship's illusion,
She'll sleep with the master, the servants, your friends,
To gratify lust, the outcome's your derision,
As from lover to enemy, she turns in the end.

At this, the Vizier began sobbing and the King had to nudge to him to keep quiet. Then it was Dirgham's turn to sing.

We slaves fear no scheme, no trick or no ruse,
Our pleasure is women to fuck as we choose.

No woman says no to a cock when she's hot,
It's your life, death and pleasure, admit it or not.

If your men have displeased you, their pricks soon delight,
For cunt's your religion and cock your insight!

When he finished singing, he jumped on top of her and she tried desperately to fend him off. The King and his men drew their swords and pounced.

The women and the slaves saw nothing but the flash of sword-blades above their heads. One slave rushed at the King but the Executioner stopped him dead with a single blow that took his head clean off.

"You still have an executioner's hand!" exclaimed the King. "May God confound your enemies and make Paradise your dwelling!"

A second slave lunged at the Executioner with a silver candle-stick-holder. He took the blow on his sword, which snapped in two. It was a fine sword and this sent him into a rage. He seized his attacker by the arms and dashed him against the wall, breaking all his bones. The King again praised his Executioner to the heavens. Realising their situation was hopeless, the slaves gave themselves up and knelt down. The King stood over them.

27

"Whoever lifts a hand will lose his head," he warned and ordered the hands of the five survivors to be tied behind their backs. Then he turned to Badr al-Budour.

"Whose wife are you and whose slave is this?"

She told him what he had already heard from Umar.

"God bless you!" said the King. "Now tell me, for how long can a woman endure sexual abstinence?"

She was taken aback at this question but he insisted that she answer.

"A woman of good family, upbringing and character," she replied calmly, "can hold on for six months. But if she's on heat, the woman lacking these and who has no self-control, gets neurotic even if there's a man on top of her with his thing inside her!"

"Whose wives are these?" he asked, pointing to the women.

"The wives of the Chief Justice, the Chief of Staff, the State Secretary, the Deputy Vizier, the Head Mufti and the Governor of the Bank."

"And the women in the bedroom?"

"They are the wives of guests, although there is one who was brought by an old woman for the slave but he hasn't done anything with her."

"That's the one I told you about, Sire," 'Umar interrupted.

"And whose wife is she?" asked the King.

"The Director of the Chamber of Commerce," she replied.

"Who are they?" he asked, pointing to the girls.

"The daughters of the Treasury Secretary, the Mayor, the State Comptroller, the Chamberlain, the Director of Education, the Secretary of Guilds and the Keeper of the Colours."

"What are they doing here?"

"Sire, that slave loves beautiful, young women. He fucks all day and he fucks all night and his dick only sleeps when he does."

"What does he eat to keep himself going?"

"Egg yolks fried in butter, Sire, with lots of honey and wholemeal bread, and nothing but the best vintage wine to drink."

"Who procures the wives and daughters of men of state for him?"

"There's an old hag who does the rounds of the upper-class neighbourhoods and pimps the most beautiful women. They come here for the money, jewellery and diamonds."

"Where does the money come from?"

She did not want to answer at first but when the King insisted, she glanced at the Vizier's wife. It was obvious whom she meant.

"I trust your witness, Badr al-Budour and believe what you've told me is true. Now, tell me about my own position."

"It is intact but had matters carried on, it would have been different."

"Are you certain of that?"

"I am," she replied.

Of course, the King was asking about his own wife and whether or not his honour had been compromised. It had not been but had he not acted when he did and if the slave had been allowed to continue on his merry way, the King's wife, too, would have ended up here.

"Who are the other slaves?" he asked.

"His friends. When there were plenty women around and he'd had enough, he used to pass them on to the others, as you saw."

"He looked after his women, didn't he? But why did you and your husband connive at the deception and not inform me?"

"Your Majesty, my husband knows nothing about any of this. For myself, I prefer the counsel of silence. You heard the song I sang, didn't you, about how a man should never trust a woman?"

"You intrigue me, Badr al-Budour. No harm will come to you but in the Name of God and His Prophet, tell me this – did that slave fuck you? It seems that no-one was safe from him."

"By God and His Prophet and the grace of Your Majesty, if I have not accepted my lawful husband, how could I accept what is unlawful?"

"I believe you but the first song you sang made me suspicious."

"I sang that for three reasons. First of all, when I saw, er... what I saw, I got excited like a mare on heat. Secondly, the Devil made my blood hot. Thirdly, I was trying to humour the slave into granting me respite until God released me from his clutches."

There was a moment's silence.

"I believe you, Badr al-Budour," said the King and added, "No-one will be spared but you."

She realised he meant that only she would not be put to death. The King then swore her to secrecy and turned to leave, whereupon the other women and the girls clamoured around her, weeping and wailing.

"You're his favourite," they sobbed, "please intervene on our behalf!"

She caught up with him at the door.

"You haven't told me what you plan to do," she said.

"My carriage will call for you tomorrow and bring you to me. The others will all be executed."

"Sire, I wish a dowry."

"Whatever you ask for will be yours."

"Promise me you will grant my request."

He gave her his word.

"I ask for your pardon for all the women and the girls. Otherwise, just think of the scandal in town."

"God give me strength!" he groaned.

Afterwards, the slaves were brought out and beheaded, all except the loutish and grim-looking Dirgham. His nose, ears and lips were cut off and his penis was chopped off and put in his mouth. He was then crucified on the highest wall of the house, with his playmates hanging beneath him. That done, the King returned to his palace.

In the clear light of morning, he sent for Badr al-Budour, who came to him looking lovelier than ever. He gave 'Umar ibn Sa'd back his mistress and made him his private secretary. The Chief of Police and Commander of the Guard were both generously rewarded. The Grand Vizier was ordered to divorce his wife and the son of his father's Vizier told to put his domestic arrangements in order and to guard his reputation better in future. He then had the old procuress brought before him.

"Who else, apart from you, carries on this trade?" he demanded.

"There are lots of old women who do what I do," she replied.

He ordered that she and all her like be executed and, in this way, uprooted the tree of depravity from his land and burned it.

This story has told of the least that can happen when women scheme and betray their husbands but the moral is that the man who drives his wife to breaking point gets himself into the most awful mess.

Chapter Three

The Repulsive Man

The kind of man who is repulsive to women is of shabby appearance, ugly to look at and has a small, limp and weedy penis. He is the type who, when he comes to a woman, has no idea how to treat her properly but mounts her without kissing or caressing her, without any sort of foreplay at all. He inserts his flaccid little thing inside her only with the greatest difficulty, jerks once or twice then hauls himself off her, taking longer to do so than he did on the job. His penis then shrivels up and away he goes. He has been described as slow to erect and quick to eject, with a small penis, leaden chest and lightweight buttocks.[7] A man like that is no use to a woman.

A large penis is a useful instrument. There was a man called 'Abbas who had an undersized member with which he was unable to satisfy his wife – a large, stout woman – and she began complaining about him to his friends. He was a poor man and she was wealthy but, despite many attempts to persuade her, she had always refused to give him any of her money. Eventually, 'Abbas visited a doctor and explained his problem to him.

"If you had a bigger penis, you would soon have control of the purse strings," the doctor advised. "Don't you know that a woman is controlled by her vagina? However, I'll prescribe a treatment for you."

He then prepared him a medication (the details of which we will give later) that enlarged his member so much that, when 'Abbas's wife saw his new condition, she was so impressed that she handed over all her money, possessions and property to him!

---

[7] Imru'l Qays, one of the greatest of pre-Islamic poets, was accused by women of these very shortcomings.

Chapter Four

The Repulsive Woman

The sort of woman men find repulsive is ugly and sullen with matted hair, a protruding forehead and dirty, slit eyes. She has a big nose, wide mouth, bluish lips and wrinkled cheeks, is gap-toothed and sprouts hairs on her chin. The sinews and veins on her wizened neck stick out, her shoulders and chest are narrow and her sagging dugs are leathery. Her belly is like an empty basin and her navel juts out like a walnut. Her ribs protrude like bows, her backbone like an iron chain and her buttocks are bony and scrawny. Her vagina is cold and loose, dirty and smelly, lumpy and bumpy and has a discharge. She has knobbly knees, spindly legs, big, flat feet and enormous hands.

A woman like that is no good at all, nor is the man who marries her or approaches her. May the Lord protect us from her and her like!

A raucous woman with a loud laugh is unattractive. It has been said that if a woman is often seen joking and fooling around then she is a slut. Similarly, there is the woman who discloses her husband's secrets and his personal business; or the one who delights in the misfortunes of others and points out the shortcomings of good, honest people, even those of her own husband; there is the woman who is never out of the neighbours' houses; the interfering busy-body and the shrew; the shrill, strident woman who never stops talking; the gossip and tell-tale; the frivolous airhead; the indolent stay-in-bed; the self-righteous harridan who loves to find fault; the hysteric, the nag and the pilfering slag; the woman who slanders and makes false accusation; the spreader of scandal and insinuation; the woman who spies and makes trouble and cheats, who schemes and tells lies and is full of deceit – that two-faced deceiver whose promise, when spoken, is her word to be broken.

You feel a sense of dread if she comes near and heave a sigh of relief when she turns away.

Chapter Five

Sexual Intercourse

If you feel the desire to make love, you should approach your wife having eaten or drunk only very little beforehand. Intercourse will then be more enjoyable, more satisfying and safer. Sex on a full stomach can have harmful consequences, such as being the cause of colic, partial paralysis or gout; at the very least, it can cause urinary difficulties and weaken the eyesight. It is much healthier to have sexual intercourse on a light stomach.

Foreplay is a necessary prelude to lovemaking. It will excite the two of you, bring you both to the same level of arousal and brighten her eyes with desire. This is more exciting for her and, indeed, healthier and more enjoyable for you.

When you have satisfied your desire, do not be in a hurry to rise from her but do so gently, on your right-hand side.

Chapter Six

Sexual Technique

When you feel the desire for intimacy, you will both find it more agreeable to perfume yourselves first. Engage in foreplay with your wife in bed, caress her and kiss her and lick her all over, on her front and her back, until you see desire quicken in her eyes. Then position yourself between her legs, insert your penis into her vagina – and do it. Foreplay beforehand will make it much more enjoyable for the two of you (as well as being gentler on your stomach).

It is said that when you wish to make love, lay your wife upon her back and hold her tight and squeeze her. Kiss her on the lips; kiss and caress her neck, breasts, belly and thighs; lick, nibble and suck her as well. Turn her around, roll her over and continue to kiss and caress her until you see she has become relaxed and aroused. Then penetrate her. In this way, the two of you will be able to reach climax together. Foreplay arouses a woman; if you neglect it, she will neither feel sufficient desire nor will she reach her climax.

When your need is spent and you wish to rise from her, do not rise directly but do so gently, on your right-hand side and, if she has conceived, the child may, God willing, be a boy. Physicians and men of learning have written on this subject:

> Let the man lay his hand upon the belly of the woman who has conceived and say, "In the Name of God and with the blessings of His Apostle, let this child be a boy and I shall name him Muhammad, after the name of our Prophet." If said with sincerity and conviction, God will create a boy, with the blessing of His Apostle.

It is not advisable to drink too much water immediately after intercourse as doing so will weaken the heart. If you wish to repeat the act, it is desirable that you both wash yourselves first.

You should be careful of letting your wife mount you because of the danger her fluids will pass into your urinary tract and cause jaundice, which can be fatal. On no account should you try to obstruct ejaculation as this will cause hernia or stones in the urinary tract. It is unwise to make energetic movements immediately after intercourse; instead, you should relax for a while. After you have withdrawn, you should allow your member to relax before washing it. The head should be washed with care. The penis should not be rubbed or washed excessively after withdrawal, as this may cause chronic inflammation and redness.

There are many and various ways to make love. The Word of God tells us *Your women are as the land you plough; go to your land as you will.*[8] You may thus enjoy a woman in whatever position you please, as all are known to be permissible.[9] For example:

- Let your wife lie upon her back and raise her thighs, take up a squatting position between them and penetrate her. This is a suitable position for the larger penis.
- The woman lies upon her back and lifts her knees up to either side of her head, so that her buttocks are raised and her vulva protrudes; then penetrate her. This position is suitable for the smaller penis.
- Have the woman lie upon her back then position yourself between her thighs, place one of her legs over your shoulder, the other under your arm and penetrate her.
- Let the woman lie upon her back and place her legs upon your shoulders; then enter her.
- While both of you lie on your side, part the woman's legs and penetrate her (however, intercourse lying on the side can cause sciatica).
- The woman gets down on her elbows and knees and you penetrate her from behind.
- Have your wife lie on her side and kneel between her thighs, place her top leg on your shoulder and the other between your thighs. She stays lying on her side as you penetrate her, at the same time hugging her to your breast and caressing her.
- Let the woman lie with her legs folded under her and place your knees one on either side of her so that her legs are between your thighs; then penetrate her.

---

[8] Quran II, 223.

[9] Khawam's version, *(op. cit.,* p. 119), adds the qualification: "... except in her rear end."

- Have her lie on a low divan or chair, either face down with her knees on the ground or with her back on the seat, her feet on the ground and her buttocks resting on the angle of the chair; then penetrate her.
- With both hands, the woman holds onto a suitably low branch of a tree. You place her legs around your waist and have her keep them there. Penetrate her while you are also holding onto the branch and the more you thrust, the more will she rock to and fro.
- Have her lie down and place a cushion or pillow under her buttocks. Spread her thighs wide and, placing the soles of her feet together, position yourself between her knees and penetrate her.

There are countless positions for lovemaking, of which I have given only a few examples here. God alone is the Giver of Success.

Chapter Seven

The Harmful Effects of Intercourse

Sexual intercourse can have a number of harmful consequences. I shall mention here only those that are the most necessary to know.

Intercourse in a standing position damages the knees and causes muscle spasms, while intercourse on the side causes sciatica. Sex before breakfast harms the back, reduces energy and weakens eyesight; doing it immediately after bathing also weakens the sight and may cause blindness. Back ache and heart pains will be provoked if a man ejaculates while lying on his back with his wife on top. Should any of the woman's vaginal fluid enter his urethra while in this position then jaundice, which can be fatal, may result. Obstructing ejaculation will cause hernia and stones in the urinary tract. Energetic movements and forceful washing of the penis too soon after intercourse will cause erysipelas. Sex with old women is a deadly sure poison.

Excessive sexual activity is harmful to bodily health. Seminal fluid derives from nourishment, much as butter derives from milk. When the butter is removed, what remains of the milk has little nutritional value. The sexual enthusiast who fails to sustain himself with adequate consumption of potions and tonics, meat, honey, eggs and the like, risks suffering fatigue, impairment of vision (if not blindness), emaciation and heart weakness. He will have no energy for the chase and if he lifts anything heavy or does any sort of physical labour, will soon become tired.

Siqilli[10] has noted, and I would concur, that optimum sexual activity for each of the four temperaments is as follows: the sanguine and the phlegmatic may copulate two or three times a month, the bilious and melancholic once or twice a month. Nevertheless, I observe that, nowadays, people of all four types tire not of copulating day and night. They are unaware that, sooner or later, such excess will give rise to illness.

The health regime a man should follow and the things he should avoid are summarised in the following verses, composed at the request of the Caliph Haroun al-Rashid[11] by Dr. Bayadiq, the most expert physician

---

[10] Siqilli: "the Sicilian"; the reference is unclear.
[11] Haroun al-Rashid: the fifth Abbasid Caliph (786-809).

of his day, with the stipulation that they be concise (not more than a page in length), easy to remember and relevant to both the man at home and the man on the road:

Don't rush or be greedy with food that you eat,
Avoid food that's tough and blood in your meat,
Chew your food well, that's advice you should follow
And if you can't chew what you're eating, don't swallow.

At meal times be careful and don't drink too quickly,
Only take drugs if you should feel sickly,
Don't hold in what nature intends you expel,
Especially at night-time, if you would sleep well.

A bath every two days is certainly best,
Avoid too much sex or your health it will test
(And sex with old women's a poisonous perversion)
– That is the advice of Bayadiq, the Persian.

Physicians are agreed that all the worst diseases afflicting the human race have their origins in sexual intercourse. Therefore, the man who would maintain his health and sight and live a contented life, let him copulate in moderation. It is otherwise the most terrible of scourges!

Chapter Eight

Names for the Penis

A mong the very many names for the male member are the following: stud, standard, organ, pigeon, jingle-bells, stroker, shifty, poker, jerk, dozy, butter, basher, knocker, thirst-quencher, screw, plunger, intruder, cyclops, weeper, long-neck, baldy, peeper, goat, grouse, cheeky, bashful, tearful, rocker, roller, ravisher, rummager, drip, tinkler, frotter, snout and scout.

In Arabic, the two basic names for it are stud (*kamara*) and standard (*dhakar*). The latter is derived from the word meaning the reputation or standing (*dhikr*) of a man. If a man's penis suffers some serious mishap – amputation or chronic impotence, for example – the Arabs say that that man's standing in the world has died and his issue has been severed. When a man dies, it is said metaphorically that his standard has fallen and his time is up.

*

A man is known by his standing in the world. It is an indication of his impending death if, in a dream, a man sees his penis cut off.

Teeth (in Arabic, *asnân*) are interpreted to mean years (*sinîn*). If a man sees a set of teeth in a dream, it means his time is up and his end is nigh.

A fingernail (*zhifr*) seen in a dream symbolises triumph (*zhafar*). A man who sees his fingernail turned upside down in a dream will experience the reversal of a previous success over an opponent. However, if he sees what looks like his opponent's fingernail turned upside down, it means he himself will now gain the upper hand.

Dreaming of a lily (*sausana*) is a sign that something unpleasant will last for a year (*sana*).

Poppies (*na'imât*) are a bad omen, since the word can be separated into the components *na'i* (announcing a death) and *mât* (died).

All sorts of misfortune will befall the man who sees *kanâfa* pastries in a dream, since this is to be understood as "be (*kun*) in misery" (*âfa*).

Roses (*ward*) in bloom indicate the impending arrival (*wurûd*) of serious news. Withered roses, however, indicate something that had previously been thought true will actually turn out to be false.

Jasmine (*yasmîn*) is to be interpreted as "despair (*ya's*, *i.e.* the opposite of hope), is untrue" (*min*). Therefore, if jasmine is seen in a dream, it suggests that despair is mistaken and that one will, in fact, get what one wants. The reasoning behind this is that jasmine is resilient and can stand up to even strong gusts of wind, whereas the slightest breeze will blow the petals off a rose. As well as the meaning that to despair is to err, dreaming of jasmine can also mean that one should be confident a wish will come true.

An earthenware marmite (*burma*) in a dream symbolises the conclusion (*inbirâm*) of some matter on which one is currently engaged. The enemy of the Prophet, Abu Jahl – God curse him – once remarked ominously, "This is a matter that will be concluded at night."

A large jar (*khâyiba*) is a sign of failure (*khayba*). However, if the jar is seen falling into a well or river, or to crack open, it is a sign of success.

Curtains (*sutûr*) seen in a dream symbolise protection (*satûr*) and mean that a man will be protected in everything he does.

Sawing (*nishâra*) indicates good news (*bishâra*).

An inkwell (*dawâya*) symbolises a cure (*dawâ'*) or relief for something but the contrary if the inkwell is broken, burned or damaged.

A turban (*'amâma*) that is seen to slip over the eyes is an indication of blindness (*'aman*) – may God protect us from it!

A bottle of eye makeup that is lost or damaged also indicates blindness, whether of the eyes or of the heart. However, if it is subsequently found, or was seen undamaged in the first place, it symbolises a cure for something, or success.

Seeing oneself climbing through a window symbolises a change of circumstances, greater or less in proportion to the size of the window. Squeezing through a very narrow window indicates an escape from the most straightened circumstances.

Dreaming of an orange (*narankh*) suggests an outbreak of fire (*nâr*) or discord in the place where the orange is seen. Trees (*ashjâr*) indicate a quarrel (*mushâjara*), carrots (*asifnâriya*) bring burning grief (*asaf nâri*). Turnips (*lift*) suggest misery (*al-âfat*), greater or less in proportion to the size of the turnip!

An empty bottle of talcum powder symbolises hidden discord or concealed mischief, whereas a full one means that the discord or mischief will take place in the open.

Fire is a bad omen.

A man having taken the pledge who sees a glass or a cup break will revert to his old ways. The broken glass of a drinker indicates that he will give up drinking, while a temperate man who sees a broken glass somehow restored will revert to his former ways.

Mice are a sign of plenty or paucity, in proportion to their number.

If one sees oneself in a dream bidding farewell or waving good-bye, absent friends will shortly return. This prompts the following verse:

> *If you dream of farewell then be joyful*
> *And let not the distance dismay,*
> *Farewell is a sign of returning,*
> *Of a homecoming soon, any day.*

Coriander (*kusbur*) seen in a dream symbolises a clean pussy (*kuss bari*). The Caliph Haroun al-Rashid was sitting one day with a group of friends when he got up to visit one of his concubines but, finding that she had her period, he came back and rejoined the group. A short while later, however, the woman's period ended. She washed and sent her maid to the Caliph with a bowl of coriander. He did not understand the intended symbolism so handed it to one of the court poets who examined the bowl and improvised the following:

> *She's sent coriander but what can it mean?*
> *Well, having considered this thing that I've seen,*
> *I take her to mean that her pussy's now clean!*

If blood is seen in a dream, there will be bloodshed, either behind closed doors or out in the open.

A drawn sword indicates confrontation; whomever is seen holding the hilt will gain the upper hand.

A bridle is a sign of bondage and domination.

A bushy beard is a sign of status and wealth, although some say that it indicates a death, if it is so long that it reaches the ground. A long beard has also been interpreted by some as a sign of diminished intelligence. There is a story about a man who saw the phrase "the longer the beard, the smaller the mind" written on the back cover of a book. Now, this man happened to have a long beard and when he read this, he took hold of his beard and put the end into the flame of his reading lamp. The flame burned off the end but also burned his hand and as he let go in pain, his whole beard went up in smoke. Suitably chastened, he wrote underneath, "Tested and true: the longer the beard, the smaller the mind!"

Another anecdote has Haroun al-Rashid in his observatory one day when he spots a man with a long beard. He orders the man brought before him.

"What's your name?" asks the Caliph.

"Abu 'Arouba," replies the man.

"And your profession?"

"I am a scholar of the law."

"In that case," says al-Rashid, "I would like your opinion on the following: a man buys a goat that then relieves itself with such force that a piece of its shit puts out one of his eyes. Who pays the damages, the buyer or the seller?"

"The seller," replies the man.

"Why?"

"Because he sold it without first telling the buyer it had a catapult up its arse!" says the man, perfectly straight-faced.

This amused al-Rashid, who made up the following verse:

> *The length of his beard and a man's rationality*
> *Are two things that stand in inverse proportionality.*

If met in dreams, the names *Hamid, Mahmoud, Hamdouna* and *Hamdoun* all indicate the happy outcome of some event. *'Ali, 'Aliya* and *'Ulya* suggest superiority and status. *Nasr, Nasir, Mansour, Nasrallah* and *Abu Nasr* indicate a victory over opponents, while *Salim* and *Salma* indicate that all one's affairs are on a sound footing. *Fathallah, Fatih* and the like suggest a forthcoming success, while *Wa'id* and *Wa'ida* indicate menace. Names with the components *latif* (kind), *mughith* (helpful), *'aziz* (dear), *hanin* (gentle) and the like, such as *'Abdallatif* or *'Abdal'aziz*, are to be interpreted in terms of the meanings of these words, for better or worse. This finds support in the words of the Prophet: "If the meaning of a dream is unclear then take the names as a guide."

However, I have digressed, so let us now return to the subject of this chapter.

*

The word "organ" is, in Arabic, etymologically related to the word for "bellows", to which it is also akin semantically, by virtue of its tumescence and detumescence: the male organ erects and goes limp like bellows inflate and deflate. "Pigeon" is a sleeping penis, brooding upon the testicles rather like that bird brooding on its eggs. "Jingle-bells" makes a ringing noise as it moves in and out. When erect, "stroker" rubs his head against the door and pushes before sinking in. "Shifty" behaves restlessly when inside, unable to stay in one place for long, until coming calms him down. With his in-and-out movements, "poker" pokes the fire. "Jerk" is a pretentious, stuck-up prick. Approaching a woman when erect, he is full of conceit at his own strength and virility and seems almost to be saying to her vagina,

"Today, my rival, I'm going to make you love me!"

Vagina trembles, terrified by his size.

"Who could possibly take all this?" she gasps.

He struts up to her door and vagina purses her lips in fear but once she finds that he's inside, she starts laughing. And when he comes, it's as if she's saying,

"You're just a little jerk! I can hardly feel you!"

You can almost hear the balls chiming in chorus, "He's dead! He's dead! He's dead!"

"I'm all right," the deflated little prick bleats indignantly as he withdraws, "there's nothing the matter with me."

Can't you almost hear him say it?!

After all his exertion, "dozy" goes limp when he withdraws then nods off to sleep. "Basher" bangs his head against the front door to force it open, in his rush to get inside. "Knocker" is just as keen but knocks politely first before making his entrance. "Thirst-quencher" apologises for the intrusion and promises to be on his best behaviour. True to his word, he won't withdraw until he's slaked her thirst. "Screw" drills his way through the door and selfishly satisfies his lust. When "plunger" dives in, he splashes and swims around left and right, this way and that. "Intruder", "peeper" and "weeper" are obvious names.

"Cyclops" has an eye unlike other eyes. "Tearful" is always shedding tears. He cries when he stands up, he cries when he sees a pretty face and he cries when he touches one. "Long-neck" also has a wide throat, a broad back, a smooth head with a protruding rim, and veins that stick out. There is not a single hair growing on "baldy's" head. "Goat" is what a short, fat penis is called, while a penis nestling among abundant pubic hair is reminiscent of a grouse nesting in the grass.

When "cheeky" gets taken hard, his behaviour is completely shameless and he starts poking around inside his owner's trousers, trying to get out. You can see his owner become more and more embarrassed – but not his impudent little penis. "Bashful", on the other hand, seldom exposes himself. "Rocker" and "roller" dance in with their balls and all when they're in the mood. "Drip" drools when hard and again when he gets inside, especially if he's been out of action for a while.

When a noise like the sound of a babbling brook is heard, you can tell that "tinkler" is on the job, particularly if he's with a well-lubricated woman. "Ravisher" is a strong and vigorous deflowerer of virgins. Not content to stay in one place, "rummager" pokes his nose into all sorts of out of the way places. According to one school of thought, "frotter" makes his entrance after rubbing his head against the vulva but another school claims he is really "limp dick" who cannot introduce himself and instead engages in frottage to make himself come. "Snout" pokes around and reaches into unusual places. "Scout" is another strong and vigorous member, a stranger to self-doubt and shame who never slackens on the job.

And so on.

Chapter Nine

Names for the Vulva

There are many names to describe a woman's vulva, including: pussy, chameleon, squeezer, sparrow, slit, bonnet, little-nose, hedgehog, taciturn, gripper, heavyweight, hisser, beast, avid, beauty, pump, little-forehead, spacious, show-case, deep-throat, gorge, thin-lips, pouter, riddler, vivacious, devoted, assistant, dome, curtains, sentry, hostess, snatch, patience, juicy, tight-fit, grotto and nibbler.

In Arabic, the principal word for vagina (*farj*) denotes, essentially, anything that can be opened. It has been claimed that the word can be applied to a man, on the basis of the Quranic verse: *Those men and women who maintain observance will be shown a way*[12] but here, "way" (*faraj*) is a different, although related, word. The word *farj* means a gap or an opening as in, for example: "I discovered a gap (*farj*) in the mountainside" and it is this word which is applied to a woman's vagina. However, in the Quranic verse, "way" (*faraj*) means "a release from suffering".

*

If a man sees a vagina in a dream, it is a sign that God will free him from any trouble he might find himself in – if he is having bad luck, it will be reversed, if he is poor, he will become rich, if he needs something, he will get it and if he owes money, he will repay it. In this way, it can be interpreted as meaning a release from suffering. It is more auspicious still if the vagina is open.

However, if it is the vagina of a virgin which is seen, it is a sign that the dreamer will not succeed in achieving what he wants since the way is blocked. Indeed, some people take this to mean that misfortune and distress are impending. At any rate, it is not auspicious. A girl's opened vagina, or at least opened at the entrance, indicates that the most difficult aim will be achieved but only after a period of disappointment; help will shortly be at hand from an unexpected source.

---

[12] Quran XXXIII, 35.

Dreaming of a man penetrating a girl and then rising from her so that her vagina becomes visible, means your aim will be achieved with the help of that man, but at a price. If you see yourself penetrating her and see her vagina, it indicates that a very difficult objective will be achieved, at least partially by your own efforts. In any event, it is an auspicious sign.

If a man dreams of himself engaged in intercourse and ejaculating, it means he will get whatever it is he wants. Dreaming of intercourse without ejaculation, however, gives a contrary indication. It is said that the active partner will get what he wants from the passive partner.

Dreaming of women with whom it is legally forbidden to have intercourse, such as mother or sisters, indicates that a man will shortly tread on sacred ground, *i.e.* ground forbidden to non-Muslims, and perhaps make the pilgrimage to Mecca and visit the holy shrines.

As mentioned above, if a man dreams that his penis has been cut off, it indicates his forthcoming death and the end of his line.

A casserole dish (*marûzîya*) indicates some misfortune (*razî'ya*) will shortly befall the dreamer.

Trousers (*sirwâl*) indicate a new appointment since the word is to be interpreted as "go (*sir*) in charge" (*wali*). A man once dreamed that the Emir gave him a pair of trousers; he was later appointed to the position of judge. Trousers also indicate modesty and the getting of something you want.

In dreams, almonds (*lawz*) are to be interpreted as meaning "coming to an end" (*ziwâl*). Consequently, they suggest an end to troubles, a cure from illness or an easing of hardship. A man who once dreamed of eating almonds asked an interpreter of dreams what it meant and was told that his current difficulties would shortly come to an end, which indeed they did!

A molar tooth symbolises an enemy and dreaming that one has fallen out indicates an enemy's death. Some people actually refer to an enemy as "a molar".

A bonnet, headscarf and slippers are associated with women and their condition gives an indication of a woman's social status and circumstances. A man who sees new slippers in a dream will marry a virgin, while used ones suggest marriage to a divorcée, of an age in proportion to that of the slippers.

Seeing something wrapped up or folded and subsequently opened suggests that a man should prepare himself for some event, good or bad, that will happen.

Quotations from the Quran or the reported sayings of the Prophet occurring in dreams are to be interpreted at face value, for better or worse.

Horses, donkeys and mules are a good sign. The Prophet said, "Good luck is bound to a horse's mane until the day of resurrection" and the Word of God itself tells us that He has created these beasts *for men to ride upon and as ornament.*[13]

A donkey seen in a dream represents a man's luck or fortune. Someone who sees himself trotting on the back of a donkey will have good luck in all his affairs. However, if the donkey stumbles or refuses to move, he will experience a setback that will be particularly severe if the donkey throws him to the ground.

Scandal will follow if a man's turban is seen to fall off his head, since the turban is the crown of the Arabs.

Walking on bare feet is a sign of the death of a man's wife, while the sight of oneself bare-headed represents the death of a parent.

You may draw your own conclusions from the above.

*

"Pussy" is the name given to the soft, voluptuous sex of a beautiful, young woman. Each and every vulva can be called a "squeezer" while "chameleon" describes the one of a very young woman. "Sparrow" is another name for the sex of a very young woman or, according to some, of a dark-skinned woman, while "slit" is a thin vulva. "Bonnet" has a frill, like a cockscomb and "little-nose" has a protruding clitoris. The hairy vulva of an older woman is a "hedgehog". "Taciturn" says very little during intercourse and "gripper" does to the penis what her name suggests and sighs whenever he enters.

"Heavyweight" is very demanding. She might associate with a procession of penises every day but if she's in the mood, she still wants more. Consequently, she is often in hot pursuit of a reluctant member that is anxious to make its exit. If her demands were less excessive, he would

---

[13] Quran XVI, 8.

be less keen to make his exit. "Hisser" is a noisy pisser. With some women, "beauty" is their most admirable feature, while with others, "beast" is their worst. When "pump" reaches climax, she goes into contractions until coming to a close. Some women are "avid" to have it and hate to let go of the member.

"Gorge" is distinguished by its width and can be satisfied only by an uncommonly large organ. "Thin-lips" has long and delicate labia, while "pouter" has very prominent labia, not unlike the rear-end of a sheep. "Riddler" shakes and stirs the member around inside her with a sieve-like action. "Vivacious" maintains an energetic and tireless exchange with the member until they come. "Devoted" is affectionate and helpful, following his movements and revealing all her hidden places to him. "Assistant" comes to the aid, in any way she can, of the organ whose climax is still some way off and so quickens his pleasure.

"Dome" is a prominent *mons veneris*, shaped like a cupola and "curtains" open between a woman's thighs when she lies down and close when she stands up, although there are some who say that this is the name for one that is clearly visible from behind. "Sentry" confronts a penis like a soldier accepting the challenge of a battle-hardened, sword-waving warrior. But our sentry is a skilful defender and takes his blows on her shield. According to some, "hostess" has a deep craving for lovemaking, while others contend she is one that is neither timid nor shy but receives her guest with a warm, friendly welcome. "Snatch" never tires and on meeting something large and hard, takes hold of him and pulls him this way and that.

"Patience" can be introduced to a series of men who enjoy her in succession but she displays great forbearance, even willingness (in fact, she thanks God for her good fortune). "Juicy" is, of course, well-lubricated, while "tight-fit" is naturally tight. "Grotto" has a wide entrance and is so deep that the penis cannot reach all the way in; there are, however, other interpretations. "Nibbler" contracts upon the member and nibbles him when she has her climax, while "little-forehead" has a prominent pubic bone. "Show-case" is a generous vulva and perineum and is quite lovely to look at. But "deep throat" is that full and voluptuous, domed and orb-like vulva. It bulges for all to see between her thighs when she sits down, especially if she sits crossed-legged and when she walks, you can see its shape beneath her clothes every time she takes a step. May the Lord in His Mercy not deny us its like! She only finds satisfaction with a large, hard, long-lasting and vigorous penis.

*

During the reign of Haroun al-Rashid, there was a man by the name of Ja'idi who had a reputation as a clown but was, nonetheless, a rather ambiguous character. Women would tease him and laugh at him but he had a high success-rate in bedding them. He was lucky with women and had their measure, as indeed he had the measure of princes and pimps, courtiers and coolies. The age seemed to produce men like him:

> *Jokers and misfits, half-wits and clowns*
> *Were produced by the age that they lived in,*
> *A whore for a wife or a pimp all his life,*
> *Or his arse, like an inkwell, much dipped-in.*

Here is a story that Ja'idi told:

"There was a neighbour of mine, a beautiful, elegant and tall woman, and I was infatuated by her. She had a marvellously voluptuous figure and it didn't seem to matter if she was walking or standing still, the mound of her pussy always showed beneath her dress. There was a group of women who used to tease me and joke with me, laugh at the things I said and fall for my stories. I used to fool around with them, kissing, squeezing, hugging and that sort of thing and every once in a while I'd fuck one of them. But this one wouldn't play. She would not even get close. Whenever I made a pass at her, she replied with this cryptic verse:

> *Between the hills I spy a tent*
> *Pitched high for all to see*
> *But a central pole it lacks,*
> *Like a leather bucket with no handle,*
> *The ropes in the middle, slack*
> *And its inside, copper-plated.*

Now, because these lines made no sense to me, I could never think up a suitably neat reply. I asked around all the well-read and educated men of my acquaintance but no-one could give me a convincing explanation.

Then one day, somebody told me that Abu Nuwas[14] was in Baghdad. So I went and paid him a visit, told him what was going on and recited her poem to him.

'This woman's heart could be yours,' said Abu Nuwas. 'And she has a marvellous body, hasn't she?'

'Terrific,' I agreed.

'And she doesn't have a husband, does she?'

'No, she doesn't.'

'Well, she thinks you've got a little dick and little dicks don't turn her on. But things are otherwise, are they not?'

I assured him they were and he then proceeded to explain the poem to me, line by line.

'When she says "between the hills", she's alluding to her thighs and "a tent pitched" is a reference to her sex. "High for all to see" tells me that when she walks, you can see its outline beneath her clothes and "a central pole it lacks" tells me that there's no husband in the picture. She's drawing a likeness here between the central pole that holds up a tent and the penis that pins down a vagina. "A leather bucket with no handle" is useless and she's likening the bucket to herself and the handle to a man, or maybe she means the bucket is her vagina and the handle is a penis. Either way it's the same.

"The ropes in the middle, slack" means that the condition of a woman without a man is like a tent that's become slack because its guy ropes have not been made tight. And when she says "its inside copper-plated", she's likening her vagina to one of those big copper pots you boil up the broth in. Stirring with a little wooden teaspoon won't get the broth to cook properly. You need a heavy paddle and a bit of elbow grease to mix it, otherwise the broth will burn and so will the fingers of the cook. Well, it's the same with this woman, my friend. You need a cock that's big and hard like a paddle and you've got to hold her tight in your arms

---

[14] Abu Nuwas Hasan ibn Hani' al-Hakami, one of the best and best-known poets of the Abbasid period, was born in Ahwaz, Persia around the middle of the eighth century and died in Baghdad, *circa* 814. He features in several of the *1001 Nights* tales. A poet "at his best in songs on wine and pederasty" he nevertheless composed on a range of themes; see *Encyclopaedia of Islam*[(2)], Vol. I, *s.v.* 'Abu Nuwas'. The attribution to him of the verses in this story is dubious.

and caress her and help her on her way with your hands. Otherwise, don't expect her to let you fuck her. What's her name, by the way?'

'Fadhihat al-Jamal.'[15]

'I'll give you a poem to recite to her and just maybe you'll get what you want. Come back afterwards and tell me how it went.'

Assuring him I would, Abu Nuwas read me this poem:

> *Fadhihat al-Jamal, my darling, light of my eye,*
> *Did you think to your verses I could not reply?*
>
> *If so, then from that you must be disabused,*
> *It was the strength of my feelings that left me confused.*
>
> *Now, folk call me crazy, a fool, rather queer,*
> *But I've something for you which is quite without peer.*
>
> *It will turn any girl who has taken its measure*
> *To a woman who'll thank me for giving such pleasure.*
>
> *In size like a pole, it's just made for your tent,*
> *Erect it, the middle now straight and unbent.*
>
> *By taking this paddle between your two thighs,*
> *It will fit in the place which between the hills lies.*
>
> *It will shake, it will stir, it will satisfy soon,*
> *For the pot made of copper needs more than a spoon.*
>
> *And your tent will no longer have ropes slack and loose*
> *While your bucket, you'll find, has at last got a use.*

I memorised it and went to call on her. She was alone.

'What brings *you* here, you degenerate?' were her opening words.

'Necessity, Madam.'

---

[15] Fadhihat al-Jamal is a nickname that means "ravishing beauty" or "scandalous beauty".

'And what might that be?'

'Shut the door and I'll tell you!'

'We're very determined today, aren't we?'

'Indeed.'

'If I shut the door and you don't tell me, what am I going to do with you?'

'Have you no imagination, Madam? Do it with me lying down!'

This rather amused her and she told her maid to shut the door. I began making my usual suggestions and, true to form, she recited those same cryptic lines. But this time I replied with the verses that Abu Nuwas had given me. After each line, she seemed to relax and unwind and stretch herself out a little more. That made me hard like... a tent pole! When she saw it, she couldn't keep her hands off it. She took hold of it and pulled me between her legs.

'Let's go through to your bedroom, darling,' I suggested.

'You son of a bitch! It's driving me wild watching it get bigger and harder and poking against your trousers. Stick it up this fat pussy that better men than you have lusted over and died before getting into! Do it now!'

'All of it? Only in the bedroom.'

'Put it up me here and now! I'll die if you don't.'

'Only in the bedroom.'

'Now! I can't wait for the bedroom.'

She lay down on her back, opened her legs and uncovered her pussy. I'm gazing at it and it's contracting like a mare's when a stallion is near. She had my cock in her hand and was kissing it but still I held back.

'For God's sake, put it up me!'

She cuddled up closer, her pussy fluttering and throbbing. Then I relented and came to her aid. She came the moment the head was inside and gave out a long, deep, guttural moan, like the braying of a donkey. She was a fair-skinned woman and her vulva was a firm, plump mound, pink in the middle. It was quite the loveliest thing I'd ever seen. And I praise the Lord that she whose pussy it was, was the loveliest of His creatures. As she lay there, I quickly slipped it in, convinced she wouldn't be able to take more than a third of it. I watched it sink in and at how she was taking it.

'Ah, how I needed this!' she gasped.

Then I pushed the whole thing in and she let out another enormous groan and began thrashing around. I'd never seen a woman behave like that before.

'Don't forget the sides and above and below and in the middle,' she was crying. 'Yes, stir it around in the middle. And when you come, do it right up inside me!'

The two of us went at it with no inhibition, blissfully fucking and hugging and kissing, giving and taking, legs intertwining before finally coming together and we collapsed exhausted, all our passion spent. I then tried to withdraw from her but she became abusive. I eventually did get it out, only to wipe it quickly and slip it back in. And off we went again. An hour later, and still without coming, we got up and went through to the bedroom where she gave me the root of some plant.

'Keep it in your mouth and your cock won't let you down.'

She told me to lie on my back while she got on top, took my penis in her hand and guided the whole thing inside her. I was amazed at how she could take it all. She's the only woman I've known who could and I'm still not sure how she did it. Perhaps it was because she was a voluptuous woman and her vagina was particularly large or deep. But maybe there was some other reason. Anyway, she starts bouncing up and down, squeezing it inside her and moaning, lifting herself up and sinking back down. ('Has he any more to give me?' she wonders, stealing a look.) She leans back and lets it almost withdraw then slides down on top and the whole thing disappears once more. And so she carried on until she came. Then she dismounted and lay down beside me, told me to lie on top of her and guided me in again.

We carried on like this until dark. At one point I tried to get up and go but she wouldn't have it and swore at me again.

'Let it rest in God's hands,' I thought, 'while I still have the strength. But may He release me in the morning!'

We went at it all night long, falling asleep once but only to doze. I think we did it twenty-seven times in all and there was one time that seemed to go on and on. I thought she'd never let me go.

When I told Abu Nuwas what had happened, he was amazed.

'My friend, that woman is too much for you. You could never handle her. She'll grind you down and spit you out quicker than all those other women put together.'

When word got out of what had happened, Fadhihat al-Jamal began looking to get married; all I was looking for was a fuck. I turned again to Abu Nuwas for advice.

'Marry her and you'll ruin your health and find yourself out in the cold with nowhere left to turn,' he told me. 'Take my advice, Ja'idi, a woman as demanding as her will wear you out and screw you up.'"

Such is the case of women who only find satisfaction with jokers, servants, misfits and drop-outs. Abu Nuwas composed the following verses about this:

> *Women are demons you never should trust,*
> *What they want most is to satisfy lust.*
> *Their purpose in love is hidden, unspoken,*
> *Deceivers, betrayers, who loves will be broken.*
>
> *If you show her a sharing and generous attitude*
> *Then one day, for sure, you will know her ingratitude.*
> *Daily she'll ask you to buy for her more*
> *But when hot, she will pick up the servants and whore.*
>
> *And when nothing is left then you can expect*
> *That everything else about you she'll reject.*
> *There's only one time when a woman is gratified*
> *And that's when her craving for cock has been satisfied.*
>
> *God save me from women and their fiendish plots*
> *And from old hags especially, the worst of the lot!*

Chapter Ten

The Members of Animals

A nimals have members that are quite unlike those of men. Those of the hoofed beasts, in particular, are enormous. The hoofed beasts include the horse, the donkey and the mule; the camel has padded feet. The cloven-hoofed beasts are the bull, the ram and certain wild animals, while the clawed beasts include the lion, the tiger, the wolf, the fox and dogs.

Names for the penises of hoofed beasts are truncheon, piston, prick, drumstick, stroker, pump, big-head, lampshade, archway, pestle and turban. The camel's is called pole, long-thing, strap, upright, plonker, pendulum, tip-top and slacker. As for the cloven-hoofed beasts, the bull's is known as nervous, hard-hat, pizzle, thin-head and long-thing, while the ram's is called stalk. Finally, the penis of the clawed beasts goes by the names of rod, piston and cosh.

The lion is said to be the most knowledgeable and astute of God's creatures in matters of copulation. He is also said to be the most jealous of all the animals. If a lioness appears, he looks her over and sniffs her before doing anything. In this way he can tell what she's been up to. If some pig has just had her, he can detect its smell on her. There are those who say that he can even smell its semen. In that case, he flies into a terrible rage, lashes out in all directions and would kill anyone who crosses his path. Then he comes around and she knows that he knows what she's been up to and she becomes terrified. She stands quite still as he comes up to her and sniffs her a second time. He lets out an awful roar that would make the mountains tremble, turns upon her, strikes her with his paw and gives her a terrible thrashing, maybe even killing her.

It is further said about the lion that he can be deceived by flattery and will turn away from anyone who exposes his private parts to him. The lion will harm no-one who appeals to the name of the Prophet Daniel as there exists a prior agreement between them to this effect. This statement is supported by the evidence of experience.

Chapter Eleven

Women's Tricks

The tricks of women are more numerous and cunning than those of the Devil himself. The Word of God tells us that *the cunning of women is great*[16], while *the cunning of Satan is weak.*[17] We therefore conclude that the cunning of women is superior.

There is the story that begins with a man infatuated by a beautiful woman. He sent her a succession of love letters but all his proposals were rejected. He got smart (so he thought) and sent her money (lots of it) but still she would have nothing to do with him. Feeling quite put out, he sat down and wept at having parted with so much cash for nothing in return. There matters remained until he aired his complaint to an old woman.

"Leave it to me and I'll see that you get what you want," she assured him.

When the old hag arrived at the woman's house, the neighbours warned her,

"You won't be able to enter the house because she has a dog in there that stops anyone entering or leaving. It's a vicious beast that goes for the face."

This news pleased the old woman, who now saw a way to hatch her scheme. She went home, prepared a bowl of bread and meat and returned with it to the woman's house. When the dog saw her coming, it made as if to attack her but seeing the bowl, it stopped, wagged its tail and sniffed the air. The old woman laid down the bowl in front of the dog.

"Eat up, my dear!" she said, stroking its back. "Oh, how I've missed you, looking for you all this time and not knowing where you were. Eat up!"

The lady of the house looked at the old hag in astonishment.

"How do you know my dog?"

Tears misted the old woman's eyes but she kept on stroking the dog's back and said nothing. The lady had to insist.

---

[16] Quran XII, 28.
[17] Quran IV, 76.

"This dog was once my best and dearest friend. One day, the two of us were invited to a wedding. She got all dressed up for it and lovely she looked too. She met a man who began making advances to her but she brushed him off. He wrote to her but she did not reply. He sent her lots of money but she still refused to go with him. Eventually he threatened,

"If you don't come to me, I'll put a spell on you and God will turn you into a dog."

"Cast your spells and have God turn me into anything you like," she mocked.

So the man put a spell on her and she really was turned into a dog – as you see."

Now, the old woman had mixed pepper with the bread and meat and as the dog gobbled it up, the pepper burned its mouth and its eyes began to water, as though the beast were crying. Observing this, the old woman burst into tears.

"I'm worried that the same thing might happen to me," the lady confided.

"Why is that?" asked the old hag, ingenuously.

"There's a man who has been after me for ages but I've never so much as looked his way. He's gone to lots of trouble and his outlay has been huge but I've told him flatly I won't do it. Now I'm afraid he'll cast a spell on me."

"Be careful, my dear, that you don't end up like your dog."

"But how can I find him and who'll be the go-between?"

"Well, you know, I could put you into credit and take a message to him."

"Please be quick before he casts a spell on me."

"I'll get hold of him today and arrange for him to meet you at my house tomorrow."

So off the old woman went, contacting the man later that same day and fixing a rendezvous for the following morning.

The next day, bright and early, the lady arrived at the old woman's house, hoping to find the man already there. There was no sign of him. She waited and waited.

"What in the name of God could be keeping him?" the old hag muttered.

As things would have it, he had been held up by some business matter. She glanced at the lady, who now looked quite distraught, and knew that the cause of her distraction was sexual.

"I don't think he's coming," the lady whined. "What am I going to do?"

"He must have got taken up with business, dear," said the hag, "but don't you worry, I'll help you out."

She covered up and went to look for the man but found neither sight nor sound of him. Then she had a bright idea.

"Why don't I find some nice young fellow to cool her heat today and I can get hold of the other one tomorrow?"

It did not take her long to come across a suitably handsome-looking man.

"This should see me all right with her ladyship," she thought.

"My boy," she grinned, "if there was a beautiful woman on heat, would you give her one?"

"If what you say is true then this gold dinar's yours," he replied.

She led him to her house – quite unaware that he was none other than the lady's husband. They reached the house and she told him to wait a moment while she went in first.

"I couldn't find your man anywhere but I've got a fellow outside who'll cool you down today and tomorrow I'll fix you up with the other one."

The lady peeked through the spy-hole at what lay in store and saw her own husband standing there in the flesh, on the point of entering. She dressed in a flash and charged at him.

"You degenerate!" she screamed, beating him on the chest. "You're your own worst enemy! You always swore blind you'd never cheat on me so what are you doing here? You're expecting a whore, aren't you? I've had old women on the look out for you and now I've got the proof! After today's display of shame, I'm filing for divorce!"

And her husband thought that she was speaking from injured innocence!

Friends, do you recognise the sort of deceit that women think up?

*

Then there is the one about the woman who had taken a shine to one of her neighbours, a pious, God-fearing and clean-living man. Time and again she tried to seduce him but all the tricks and schemes she cooked up failed to tempt him. It was the wrath of God that frightened him, he claimed. Then, one night, she told her maid to leave the door unlocked.

"I'm going to set a trap for our neighbour tonight," she announced.

She waited until midnight.

"Go out to the street," she told the maid, "and knock hard on the front door with a stone. I will start screaming and shouting. When you hear the sound of street doors opening, come inside and do the same on the inside door. Be careful nobody sees you and when you hear people coming, get yourself back here."

Now, this neighbour of hers was a good and decent man, a righter of wrongs who never refused to answer a call for help. When he heard the sound of banging and shouting, he asked his wife what it could be.

"It must be burglars at the neighbour's house," she replied.

He rushed to his neighbour's aid like a shot but no sooner was he inside her house than the maid locked the door and the two of them took hold of him and started screaming.

"What do you think you're doing?" he cried, bewildered.

"If you don't do you know what with me, I'm going to tell the world I owed you money and that you made me do it with you."

"Let the will of God be done," he sighed. "His command cannot be challenged nor His wisdom questioned."

Still, he tried to talk her out of it but she was having none of that and began screaming again. This brought a crowd of people to her door, which made him seriously worried.

"All right, just hide me and I'll do whatever you want."

"If you want to save your skin, climb into the closet and shut the door behind you. Otherwise I'll tell them that you screwed me but I prevented you from leaving."

Realising he had no choice, he shut himself in the closet. She locked him in and went outside to calm the crowd. Once they had drifted away, she locked all the doors and kept him imprisoned for a week. She only let him go after she'd worn the poor man out!

Such is the chicanery of which the fairer sex is capable!

*

Another story concerns a woman who loathed her husband on account of his small appendage, lack of effort and premature ejaculation. He was also very ugly. She was a well-endowed woman with a vagina to match but no man had ever aroused her; in fact, she cared little for men or their company.

Now, her husband was a porter and had a donkey to carry for him. At night, the wife used to take out the donkey's straw and would be gone for a while. If her husband asked what had kept her, she would reply that the donkey was sick and she had sat down beside it until the beast had eaten. He thought nothing of it because he usually came home tired, had supper then went to bed immediately and was happy to leave the feeding of the donkey to his wife.

In fact, this woman (may God lay bare her shame) had the hots for the donkey. When it came time for its feed, she used to go outside and fasten its basket on her back, mix a little of its excrement and urine together and rub it between her legs. On her hands and knees she would crawl towards the donkey and turn around in front of it. Smelling her from behind, the donkey – not unreasonably – supposed her to be another beast of burden and proceeded to mount her. Taking the beast in hand, she guided the head of its penis in slowly, which stretched her enough for the donkey to ease itself, inch by inch, inside. In this way and for no short time, she took her leisure and her pleasure, undisturbed, with the donkey.

One night, the husband woke up abruptly with an appetite for his wife. Finding the bed empty, he rose and quietly made his way outside, where he was confronted by the sight of his wife with the donkey jogging to and fro on top of her.

"What's going on here?" he gasped.

"God damn the porter who neglects his donkey!" she screamed, scrambling up from down below.

"What are you talking about?"

"When I brought the straw and the beast refused to eat, I knew it must be unwell. I stroked its back, felt it was bent and reckoned that maybe its load is too heavy. So I strapped its basket onto my own back, by way of experiment, and discovered that I was right. It's far too much for the poor thing to carry and that's why it's been so poorly. Unless you want your donkey to collapse, carry some of its load yourself!"

Readers, just look at what women will do!

*

Two men were living in the same apartment. One had a large and vigorous member while the other, *au contraire*, possessed a thin and flaccid one. The wife of the former would rise every morning, glowing and radiant, full of good humour and fun while the wife of the latter woke up bad-tempered and out-of-sorts. The two women often sat together and talked about their husbands.

"I'm so lucky," beamed the first wife. "My bed is a happy one and our sex life one of blissful give and take. When my husband penetrates me, it's like he plugs me and when he's fully erect, he reaches all the way inside. He never pulls out until he's been all around the box and we always come together."

"I'm miserable," confessed the second. "My bed is unhappy and our sex life a tale of drudgery and hard labour. My husband's thing is too small and thin to stretch me and fill me or get very far inside at all. If he ever erects, he soon goes limp and even if he does get it in, he never comes and neither do I. He's useless as a man and as a lover."

This was how the two women talked until, one day, it occurred to the unfortunate wife to fornicate with the other one's husband.

"I have to do it with him, even if only the once," she thought.

She bided her time until, one night, her husband was not at home. She dabbed on a little perfume and, around midnight, crept into her neighbour's bedroom. Feeling in the dark with her hand, she found a space and slipped into bed between them. The husband turned over and she settled in. Both the man and his wife thought that the newcomer was the other.

She waited until the wife was fast asleep then cuddled up to the husband. The scent of her perfume aroused him and he put his arms around her.

"Let me be!" she said.

"Be quiet or you'll waken the children," he whispered, thinking that she was his wife.

"They're still awake, so don't make a sound," she murmured, afraid that his wife might wake up.

He squeezed her tight, caressed her plump, soft pussy and mounted her.

"Take it in your hand like you always do."

She took hold of it, delighted at how big it was and guided him inside her. Then she made love to him as his wife had never done. She, likewise, had never had it like that from her own husband.

"I wonder what's brought this on?" thought the man, bemused.

He did it with her one more time then, surprised but satisfied, he fell asleep. She slipped quietly out of bed and crept back to her own room.

The next morning, the husband said to his wife,

"Darling, it was wonderful last night and your perfume was so arousing."

"What is this 'it' that happened last night? And what perfume? I don't have any. It must have been a dream!"

The poor man did not know what to think!

There is no limit to women's cunning. They could get an elephant up for a ride on an ant's back!

Chapter Twelve

Questions & Answers for Men & Women

This chapter contains useful information, unavailable in other books. It deals with secret truths about women. Knowledge is better than ignorance and although knowledge may be uncomfortable, ignorance is still more so.

The story is told that Mu'abbira, reckoned to be the most worldly-wise woman of her day, was once asked,

"Where is a woman's reason located?"

"Between her legs."

"And her pleasure?"

"In the same place."

"And her love or loathing for a man?"

"Inside her vagina. If a woman loves a man, she will give him her vagina unreservedly but if she dislikes him, she will deny him. A woman will do all that she can for the man she loves and try to satisfy him in every possible way, no matter how trivial. She accepts him as he is, even if he is penniless. But if a woman dislikes a man, she will keep him at a distance, no matter how rich he would make her."

"And where is the place of a woman's perception, her passion and discernment?"

"In her eye, her heart and her vagina."

"Would you explain that?"

"Perception resides in the eye, passion in the heart and discernment, or taste, in the vagina. If a woman's eye spots a handsome man and is pleased by what it sees then affection and desire will penetrate her heart and passion, too, may find a dwelling there. The woman tracks the man of her desire and sets traps for him. If she succeeds and makes sexual contact, her vagina tastes him and her taste discerns his sweetness or his bile. A woman's discernment is in her vagina and there, by taste, she knows the good man from the bad."

Then she was asked,

"What kinds of penis do women like most? What kind of woman enjoys frequent lovemaking? What kind of woman prefers infrequent lovemaking?   What kind of man is most attractive to women and what kind is least attractive?"

"Women differ in respect of their vaginas, their lovemaking and what they find attractive and unattractive in men.   As women differ in physical stature so, likewise, do they differ in character. Men, too, differ in respect of their penises, their lovemaking and what they find attractive and unattractive in women.

The woman whose vagina is shallow enjoys the short, wide-calibre penis that fills her without going too far. She will find the longer penis uncomfortable.   However, a woman with a deep vagina enjoys the attentions of a well-endowed man, of the sort that will fill her completely. She will have no inclination towards the short, narrow penis, which will not excite her sexually.

The temperaments of women are: bilious, melancholic, phlegmatic, sanguine or a combination of these. Women of the two former temperaments do not enjoy frequent lovemaking and are compatible only with men having the same temperament.   Women of the latter two temperaments enjoy frequent and regular intercourse. If such a woman becomes aroused, she is insatiable! However, only a man of the same temperament will be compatible with her.   If a man and woman of opposing temperaments marry, they will both be miserable and unhappy. Women of mixed temperament display characteristics of both types.

The woman of short stature enjoys regular and frequent intercourse – more frequently, at any rate, than a tall woman.   She is compatible with the well-endowed man, the like of whom will gladden her bed and lighten her life.

Men are similar to women in respect of frequency of intercourse and with regard to temperament.   However, women appear to be more enamoured with a man's penis than men are with a woman's vulva."

She was then asked to say something about the worst sorts of women.

"The worst sort of woman is one who would, for example, use her own money to buy dinner then object if anyone else ate. There is the type who digs up and discloses matters you would rather remained private. There is the envious woman or the loud, shrill woman who raises her voice above her husband's, the gossip and malicious woman, the sullen, scowling woman, the hussy who makes a show of her beauty and charms and the trollop who is never at home. The woman who is often seen laughing or standing at folk's doors is a slut. There is the busy-body and the nag, the scheming or spiteful woman and the light-fingered woman who pilfers her husband's money and her friends' belongings.

There is the slovenly, the frivolous and the ungrateful woman, the woman who avoids the marital bed or who initiates lovemaking with her husband and then puts him off, or the two-faced, lying, disloyal and deceitful woman There is the troublemaker and the shrew, or the dreary woman who thinks the worst of others, the loud-mouthed and pretentious woman and the dull, simple-minded woman.

Take it from me – these are the worst sorts of women."

Chapter Thirteen

The Causes & Stimulation of Sexual Desire

Sexual desire has six principal causes: youthful ardour, an abundance of seminal fluid, proximity to the object of desire, facial beauty, good eating and bodily contact. There are eight things that enhance performance and increase sexual pleasure: good health, a carefree heart, a clear conscience, happiness, the right kind of food, a variety of partners, variety in the skin colour of partners, and lots of money.

There also exists a number of aphrodisiac preparations. For example, crush a few small pearls, mix with oil and clear honey and take on an empty stomach. Alternatively, dab the penis and vulva with wolf's bile to achieve a similar effect.

Galen wrote that a man experiencing lack of sexual energy should take a glass of thick honey, twenty almonds and one hundred pine nuts for three consecutive nights before going to sleep.

Try ground onion seeds, sifted or strained and mixed with honey; a spoonful to be taken on an empty stomach. The melted fat from a camel's hump, wiped on the penis prior to intercourse, has a remarkable effect and your partner will be well pleased.

Chewing a little cubeb (which is like a large cardamom) and rubbing it on the head of the penis just before intercourse, produces heightened pleasure for both the man and woman. The use of balsam oil has a similar effect.

Mix finely ground pelleter[18] and dried ginger with oil of lily and wipe on the penis and scrotum. This will enhance the pleasure of love-making.

To enhance your own pleasure, stimulate the production of seminal fluid and increase the potency and frequency of erection, swallow

---

[18] Pelleter, or Pellitory of Spain (*anacyclus pyrethrum*): the root of a plant native to North Africa, a little thicker than a pencil, gnarled and chocolate-coloured on the outside, white inside, with a strong and fizzy, bitter-sweet taste.

a little hashish,[19] about the size of a mustard seed. This has a particularly stimulating effect upon the ability to erect.

If you wish to enhance your wife's pleasure, chew some cubeb and pelleter together and rub the mixture on your penis before intercourse. She will love you all the more for it! Wiping the member with donkey's milk likewise has a strong effect.

Cook chick-peas and onions together thoroughly and sprinkle with a little powdered pelleter and ginger. Eat a satisfying amount of this and you will find that sexual pleasure becomes wonderfully intense.

---

[19] The word in the Arabic text, *tâkût*, is unknown to dictionaries or respondents but is phonetically similar to a dialect word for hashish.

Chapter Fourteen

Remarks on Female Sterility
&
Methods of Treatment

Doctors have studied the perplexing subject of barrenness at great length and each has concluded, in his own way, that many and various factors are involved.

For example, a woman may suffer pain and aggravation of the uterus as a result of menstruation or the retention of fluid after a period of sexual abstinence. She may suffer from the retention of menstrual blood, constriction of the uterus, dryness or inflammation, obstructed gasses or a menstrual imbalance. Other causes include spells cast by witches and the mischief of demons and jinn.

In the case of a stout woman, particularly if her husband is not well-endowed, the sperm may not reach the uterus and therefore intercourse will be unproductive.

The method of treatment is as follows: after washing at the end of her period, the woman should fit to herself a cotton cloth in which some camel's bone-marrow has been wrapped. Prepare a mixture of vinegar and a measure of ground and sieved black nightshade; she should drink a little of this every day for seven days on an empty stomach then proceed to intercourse. A small measure of sesame oil may also be taken, after washing, at the end of her period. A bean-sized amount of red arsenic may be added to the remainder of the above mixture and taken for a further three days, prior to intercourse. God willing, this will be effective.

Another treatment is to mix borax with the bile of a sheep or cow, together with a little musk and melilot; this should be wrapped in a small towel and worn by the woman after she has washed at the end of her period and prior to intercourse.

Chapter Fifteen

The Causes of Male Sterility

A man's sperm may degrade as a result of coldness of temperament, incontinence, chills, or fever. Some men suffer from a misshapen urethra which causes ejaculation to be directed downwards and away from the womb, while there are others whose members are not long enough to reach the neck of the womb. Premature ejaculation, with the consequent failure to achieve simultaneous climax, results in infrequent conception. There are men who are chronically impotent and have extremely small penises. Additionally, a man may be affected by sudden temperature changes and other analogous factors.[20]

The degradation of sperm as a result of coldness of temperament, incontinence, chills, etc., premature ejaculation, a short penis or the affliction of the penis or bladder with sores, are all conditions that may be receptive to the proper treatment. Warming medications are indicated, such as preparations of honey, ginger, pelleter, garlic, cinnamon,[21] nutmeg, cloves, cardamom, ash seeds, pepper and other spices.

However, chronic impotence, a misshapen urethra and the like, are not treatable and the sufferer should not distress himself. Blessing lies with God alone to grant or to withhold.

---

[20] This sentence could be interpreted as: "Additionally, a man may be affected by marital discord or other similarly upsetting circumstances."

[21] Two varieties of cinnamon are mentioned: *cinnamomum zeylanicum* and *cinnamomum cassia.*

Chapter Sixteen

Ways to Provoke Miscarriage

There exists a large number of drugs and treatments that will provoke miscarriage. I shall describe here only those which I know are effective, in order to give a wider understanding of their benefits and side-effects.

A fresh madder root (or a dried one, crushed and moistened) introduced into the vagina, will destroy the man's sperm and cause the foetus to abort but may also give rise to menstrual problems. A similar effect will be obtained if the root is boiled and the infusion drunk on an empty stomach. The fumes of burning cabbage seeds, passed into the vagina through a tube, will cause the foetus to abort. A little alum placed in the vagina or rubbed on the penis prior to intercourse has a contraceptive effect but too frequent application will result in the woman's permanent sterility. Tar obtained from resinous plants, wiped on the penis prior to intercourse, is an extremely effective contraceptive and, if the woman is already pregnant, will cause the foetus to be stillborn. However, prolonged use will result in sterility.

Drinking rhubarb juice mixed with a little pepper and myrrh will provoke a copious menstruation that will flush any clotted blood from the uterus. If the woman is pregnant, it will cause her to miscarry and if in confinement, will expel placenta and cleanse the uterus. If a solution of cinnamon and red myrrh is drunk and a tampon soaked in the solution then inserted into the vagina, the foetus will abort. Similarly, an infusion of yellow rue petals, gently simmered and then drunk, will abort the foetus and expel the placenta.

All the above are tried, tested and effective methods.

Chapter Seventeen

Treatment for Three Types of Erection Problem

There are three kinds of problem relating to erection: failure to erect, failure to maintain an erection and premature ejaculation.

Regarding the first case, finely grind together the following: galingale, cinnamon,[22] Indian *harhar,*[23] cloves, nutmeg, cubeb, ash seeds, Persian pepper, Barbary fig buds, cardamom, laurel seeds, carnation petals and pelleter. Add to a bouillon, preferably of chicken, and allow to infuse thoroughly before drinking. Alternatively, the mixture may be stirred into honey and taken in the morning and evening. This is the most effective treatment available.

For premature ejaculation, stir ground nutmeg and frankincense into honey; a teaspoonful to be taken at a time.

For failure to maintain an erection, grind together pelleter, hellebore seeds, a little euphorbia, green ginger, cinnamon and cardamom, and mix with honey; again, a teaspoonful to be taken at a time This will cure the problem of maintaining an erection and all related difficulties.

These are tried, tested and effective treatments.

---

[22] Three varieties of cinnamon are mentioned: as note 21, above, plus *cinnamomum culilawan.*

[23] unknown; possibly a variety of juniper: *juniperus oxycedrus.*

Chapter Eighteen

How to Enlarge & Expand the Smaller Penis

This chapter is concerned with penis enlargement and will be of interest to women as well as men. Women are not aroused sexually by a small member or by one that is limp and weak. A woman's delight is a large and hard penis.

The poorly-endowed man who wishes to enlarge and invigorate his member should, prior to intercourse, massage it in lukewarm water until the blood circulation increases and it reddens and erects. He should then wipe it with a confiture of honey and ginger and proceed to intercourse. His wife will then experience such pleasure, she will barely allow him to dismount!

Grind and sift equal amounts of pepper, spikenard, musk and galingale and mix with the above confiture of honey and ginger. Apply this to the penis after it has been well massaged in lukewarm water and the effect will be to expand and harden the member and greatly pleasure the woman.

Alternatively, massage the member in lukewarm water. Smear a strip of parchment with hot pitch and wrap around the now erect penis. Wait until the pitch cools and the penis subsides. Repeating this procedure several times will enlarge and harden the member.

Fill a bottle with leeches, cover with oil and place in the sun until the heat produces an infusion. Rub this on the penis for several consecutive days and a similar effect will be obtained.

Chapter Nineteen

How to Remove Underarm & Vaginal Odour
&
Tighten the Vagina

Unpleasant odours in the vaginal and underarm areas and a loose vagina are most distressing conditions. To remove vaginal odour, sift powdered red myrrh, mix to a paste with an infusion of myrtle and wipe on the vagina. Alternatively, soak a small towel in a solution of sifted spikenard and rose water and place on the vagina. This has a warming effect and will remove any unpleasant odour.

To tighten the vagina, the woman should wipe thoroughly, first with a solution of alum and then with an infusion of *suek*.[24]

To cause a distended uterus to retract, simmer cored carob beans and pomegranate peel together in water then remove from the heat. The woman should squat in this for as long as she can bear. When it cools, it should be re-heated and she should resume her position. Repeat several times, fumigate with cow dung and the desired result should be obtained.

To remove underarm odour, pound antimony and mastic resin together until compact. Place in a bowl, add a little water and stir until hot. Rub the resulting paste on the underarm area and it will absorb and remove any odour. This treatment has been applied on many occasions and has always been effective.

---

[24] *Suek* is the astringent bark of the *arâk* tree (*capparis sodata*).

Chapter Twenty

The Symptoms of Pregnancy
&
How to Determine the Sex of the Unborn Child

The indications of pregnancy are well known: the woman experiences vaginal dryness from the time that her husband withdraws, she becomes listless and tired and begins to sleep heavily, the entrance of her vagina contracts so much that even an eye-pencil could barely be inserted and her nipples darken in colour. Confirmation comes when her periods cease.

If the woman's complexion and colouring remain clear and her nipples become more distinct, if her face takes on a lovely radiance, without freckling or blotching, it suggests she will give birth to a boy. The following symptoms give the same indication: prominence of, or discharge from, the right nipple, a heaviness on the right side, bleeding from the right nostril and reddening of the nipples.

Indications that she will give birth to a girl are: freckling or blotching and a sallow complexion, pains in the uterus, darkening and swelling of the nipples, heaviness on the left side and bleeding from the left nostril.

The above information has been taken from the writings of physicians whose conclusions are based upon established observation.

Chapter Twenty-One

The Benefits of Eggs
&
Sexually Stimulating Beverages

This chapter contains extremely useful information on how to enhance sexual prowess and will be of interest to men of all ages.

It is said that a daily breakfast of egg yolks is a stimulant to love-making, as is eating egg yolks with chopped onions for a period of three days. Peeled asparagus fried in butter with egg yolks and mixed spice will, if consumed regularly for three days, greatly stimulate desire and enhance performance. Similarly, chopped onions, egg yolks and mixed spice fried together in oil and eaten regularly over several days, will produce a quite indescribable improvement in prowess.

The man who drinks camel's milk and honey regularly will notice a marked improvement in performance; his member will not go to sleep, day or night. Egg yolks grilled with giblets, pepper and cinnamon will, if eaten regularly for several days, enhance prowess and help maintain a vigorous and tireless erection.

Should a man be taken by a sudden and unexpected desire to copulate all night long without having had time for the above, we suggest the following: cook a sufficiently large amount of eggs in butter or ghee, cover with honey and mix well together. Eat with bread and the member will not experience fatigue that night.

*

For thirty days and thirty nights
Stood Abu'l Hayloukh's cock upright,
He sustained himself on meat and onions
– What a credit was he to his companions!

In a long, hard night of fornication
Abu'l Hayja performed the defloration
Of eighty virgins – on a diet of chick-peas
With camel's milk and the honey of bees!

75

To fifty nights and then one score
Of non-stop fucking, Maymoun swore
And all this time, so it's been said,
He munched on egg yolks and brown bread!

Although the celebrated story of the debauched exploits of Abu'l Hayja, Abu'l Hayloukh and Maymoun the slave is farfetched and fantastic, we shall relate it here to conclude the lesson.

In the dim and distant past, a long, long time ago, there was a great and powerful king who was master of a vast army and retinue. This king had seven daughters, each one a marvel of beauty and charm, elegance and grace. Each had her own splendid palace with servants and slaves to provide for her every need. The girls dressed in men's clothes, rode horses harnessed in gold, carried swords and spears and stood against men in the field of battle – but there was not a husband between them. When the princes of the day came to propose marriage and their father asked his daughters for their decision, the answer was always a defiant and dismissive "Never!"

People took sides. There were some who spoke well of them and others who cast suspicion but, in truth, no-one knew anything about them. So matters remained until their father died and the eldest daughter succeeded to the throne. As her subjects came to swear allegiance, the truth about the girls spread throughout the land. Starting with the eldest, their names were: Fawz, Sultanat al-Aqmar, Badi'a, Warda, Mahmouda, Kamila and Zahra. Although the youngest, Zahra was the cleverest and smartest of the seven. And she loved to hunt.

Out on the chase one day, she crossed paths with a horseman and his twenty slaves. They greeted each other but the horseman could not tell if she was a woman or a man. It was a woman's voice he heard but her face was veiled. He asked one of her slaves and was given the full story.

The two engaged in polite conversation until lunchtime, when they sat down together. He had hoped to see her face then but she claimed to be fasting and declined to eat. Still, as he gazed at her hands, her eyes and figure, he was smitten by her charms.

"Do you have a partner or perhaps a good friend?" he inquired.

"The friendship of a man is not proper for a woman," she replied. "When a man and a woman become close, fantasy and temptation fill their hearts and their affair comes to everyone's notice."

"Can there not be friendship with openness and honesty, without deception and intrigue?"

"A woman's friendship with a man soon sets tongues wagging, bringing ruin to her and misery to him."

"Our friendship could be quiet and very discreet and right here, in this place, we two could meet."

"That is quite out of the question. It would create only rumour and insinuation."

"An affair between us would be the joy of congress and union, of exchange and communion of souls and possessions."

"Your words are inviting and your smile is so sweet but now say no more lest you be indiscreet."

"You've stated your case with exquisite grace but your love in my heart has now found its place. If you leave me, for sure it is death I will face!"

"Let us both go home," she smiled, "and God knows, we may, one day, meet again."

Bidding each other farewell, they set off on their separate ways.

He, however, was not the type to wait patiently. He lived in an isolated palace in a distant land where his father was a very wealthy businessman by the name of Khayroun. The son's name was Abu'l Hayja and between his palace and the girl's was a full day's journey.

When night fell, he rose, dressed and fastened his sword. On a swift horse and in the company of one of his slaves, name of Maymoun, he stole out quietly into the darkness. The two rode all night until, just before dawn, they reached a cave in the hillside. Leaving his slave there with the horses, Abu'l Hayja approached Zahra's castle on foot but, finding it heavily fortified, he returned to the cave from where he watched its comings and goings until midnight. Then, resting his head on his slave's knee, he fell asleep.

Suddenly he was awoken by Maymoun.

"Sir, there's a noise coming from the back of the cave!"

He rose, and by the dawn's early light the two of them made for a second cave a short distance away.

"Wait here while I find out what's going on," he told Maymoun.

Abu'l Hayja returned to the first cave and crept up to the back, where he discovered a passage, at the far end of which a light shone through the gaps in some debris. Putting his eye to a gap, he peered inside. There he saw Zahra, carousing with close on one hundred nymphs, in a marvellous underground palace! The floor was covered with a dazzling array of carpets and rugs on which the girls were frolicking in a lewd and wanton fashion.

"Blimey!" he gasped. "I need a helping hand."

He left them to it and made his way back to Maymoun.

"Look sharp and fetch my comrade in arms, Abu'l Hayloukh!"

Now, this Abu'l Hayloukh was the Grand Vizier's son and one of Abu'l Hayja's oldest and greatest friends. In their day, there was no-one braver or stronger in the fight than Abu'l Hayloukh, Abu'l Hayja and Maymoun the slave. They were hard men without equals.

Arriving at Abu'l Hayloukh's, Maymoun told him the story.

"*We are God's and unto Him we shall return*," said Abu'l Hayloukh, piously. "So Abu'l Hayja needs a friend to help him, does he?"

Mounting up and taking his best slave for company, he rode to the cave.

The two friends greeted each other then Abu'l Hayja told Abu'l Hayloukh about his infatuation with Zahra and how he had planned to raid her castle but had discovered instead that it was connected by an underground passage to this cave. His account of the goings-on inside appealed enormously to his friend. When night fell and the sound of laughter and raised voices could be clearly heard, Abu'l Hayja said,

"Now go take a look and you'll see why I sent for you!"

Abu'l Hayloukh crept up and peered inside. He stared in rapture at the beauty on display.

"Which of these fillies is Zahra?" he asked at last.

"The one with the stunning figure and the pouting lips, raven-haired and rosy-cheeked, a jewelled tiara on her head and a golden dress upon her breast. She's sitting on a chair inlaid with gold and silver, leaning her chin upon her hand."

"Yes, I see her. She stands out among the rest like a sceptre. But let me tell you something, brother, of which you seem to be unaware."

"Yes?"

"This place is a brothel, no doubt about it, and these girls come here at night to carouse in privacy and engage in their own queer orgies of depravity. If you thought you could get your hands on Zahra in any other place, you'd be very wrong, my friend. Sending her letters or a go-between will get you nowhere."

"Why not?"

"Oh brother!" Abu'l Hayloukh sighed. "Because it's girls she likes! That's why she's never been interested in men."

"My friend, I called you because I value your opinion and I wanted you to see this with your own eyes and give me your advice."

"If the Lord in His mercy had not guided you to this spot, you would have had no chance at all with her. From here, however, we should be able to find a way inside."

In the morning, the slaves were ordered to dig away some of the debris to make an opening, while the horses were taken to the nearby cave and penned in as a precaution against wild animals and thieves. The two masters and two slaves then returned and made their way, armed, into the palace.

Replacing the debris behind them, they were suddenly in darkness. Abu'l Hayloukh struck a flint and lit one of the candles and they began their exploration. They found an abundance of wonderful things. Carpets and cushions of every colour, furnishings and tapestries, fine chandeliers, and tables laid heavy with food, drink and fruit. Dazzled by it all, they started counting the rooms until, at the far end, they came to a large door, with a smaller door set inside it. It was locked.

"This must be how they enter," said Abu'l Hayloukh. "Come on, let's hide ourselves in one of the rooms!"

Inside a very grand room and well out of sight, they concealed themselves.

When night fell, the small door suddenly opened and in came a maidservant, carrying a candle. She lit all the chandeliers, arranged the divans and cushions, set the tables, laid out the wine and perfumed the room with incense. An hour later at most, in strolled the girls, laughing and rolling their hips as they walked. Food and drink were served and the carousing and revelry began. When the wine had clearly taken effect, the four men, armed and masked, emerged from their hiding place and stood over them.

"And who might these night intruders be?" sighed Zahra. "Have you sprung up from the ground or dropped down from the sky? What is it that you want?"

"A fuck," demanded Abu'l Hayja.

"With whom?"

"With you."

"How do you know me?"

"We met out hunting."

"Who let *you* in here?"

"The Lord, in His mercy."

Zahra considered her position. She had by her side the girls – impregnable virgins one and all[25] – and a companion, Mouna, who had never been aroused by a man in her life.

"Why don't I save myself and outsmart this gang by putting them to use?" she mused.

"All right," said she, "but only on my terms."

"Accepted in advance," they replied as one.

"And if you fail, you will be my prisoners, to do with as I please."

"Agreed."

She then made them swear to a binding agreement which was sealed with Abu'l Hayja's handshake.

"Your task," she told him, "is to deflower eighty of these virgins tonight, without coming once."

"I accept," replied Abu'l Hayja.

"What is this slave's name?" she asked.

---

[25] "Impregnable" does not do justice to the meaning of *muṣaffaḥât*, which appears in the original to describe the girls. It is, in fact, a reference to the ritual of *tasfîḥ*, still practised in rural areas of the Maghrib countries to maintain a girl's virginity intact. The practice may vary between regions but involves making a number of small incisions just above the right knee of a young girl and having her repeat a given formula. This is said to have the effect of making it physically impossible for a man to enter her until, a few days before her marriage, the ritual is repeated with the incisions – which must be performed by the same person – made in the same place and the formula reversed. See M. Chebel, *L'esprit de sérail* (Paris: Editions Payot, 1995), p. 79, who, nevertheless, has not spotted Nafzawi's reference.

"Maymoun."

"He shall fuck this woman here," she said, pointing to Mouna, "for fifty nights in a row without wilting. He can come if wants to but he must not go limp."

Everyone present was staggered by this demand but Maymoun accepted without hesitation. You see, fucking was his forte.

"And you, what's your name?" continued Zahra.

"Abu'l Hayloukh."

"Well, Abu'l Hayloukh, you are going to stand in front of the women and girls for thirty days and thirty nights while maintaining a constant erection."

Turning to the fourth, she asked his name.

"Fallah," he replied.

"You will be our servant and bring us whatever we require."

To avoid any accusation of bad faith on her part, she asked each one what he wanted by way of sustenance. Abu'l Hayja ordered camel's milk and honey, with no added water, and chick-peas and meat cooked with plenty of onions. Abu'l Hayloukh requested meat with lots of onions and, to drink, onion juice with honey (the recipe for this will be given later). Maymoun asked for egg yolks and wholemeal bread. Everyone received what he asked for.

Then, instructed to let Zahra know if he flagged, Mouna disappeared into a bedroom with Maymoun. Abu'l Hayja was shown into another room where, one after the other, eighty virgins were dispatched to him. He took each one in turn and not once did he come. Everyone was highly impressed at his outstanding performance.

"I've done what you asked for, Zahra, now keep your side of the promise."

"Not so fast! The deal applies to you all. If each of you fulfils his side of the bargain, you'll get what you want but if one slips up, you all do."

So he sat down with the women and girls to eat and drink and wait for his companions to finish.

At first, Zahra was confident they would soon be at her mercy and as each day passed and her anticipation grew, she seemed to become more radiant and lovely. Until the twentieth day, when all that changed and she started getting worried. On the thirtieth day, she burst into tears. It was then that Abu'l Hayloukh discharged himself with honour and came to join his friend in a drunken feast of celebration. Zahra now pinned her hopes on the wilting of Maymoun's resolve. Each day she sent to Mouna to ask about him but the reply was always the same:

"He gets stronger by the day! I think they're going to lick us!"

Changing tack, Zahra announced slyly,

"I've asked about the slave and am told that he is weakening."

"If he doesn't go all the way and, what's more, top it with an extra ten days, I'll kill him with my own hands!" promised Abu'l Hayja.

Maymoun kept it up for fifty days and fifty nights at which point Mouna, worn out and exhausted, heaved a deep sigh of relief. But when the fifty days had passed and he still kept on going, she sent a distress call to Zahra,

"Mistress, he's gone over the fifty days now but there's no sign of him getting off me. For God's sake get me out of here! I've been stretched apart so much that I'm unable to sit down!"

However, not only did Maymoun carry on for the extra ten days but added a further ten of his own. Everyone was enormously impressed.

So, in the end, the four men took possession of everything in the palace – money, girls, women and servants – which they divided equally among themselves. This was the incident which inspired the preceding verses.

*

The following sexually stimulating beverage carries medical endorsement:

Take one part of the juice of crushed onions to two parts clear honey. Mix well together and simmer over a low heat until the onion juice evaporates and the residue has the original consistency of the honey. Remove from the heat, allow to cool and store in a bottle. As required, mix one ounce of this with three ounces of water in which chick-peas have been soaked for twenty-four hours. Drink a little before retiring in winter and the night will not be a quiet one. With regular consumption, the member will stay tirelessly erect and hard. However, it should not be drunk by persons of hot temperament, as it may cause fever, and only the older man and persons of cool temperament should drink it for more than three successive days. It should not be taken in summer.